Travellers' Spanish

David Ellis is Director of the Somerset Language Centre and co-author of a number of language books

Rosa Ellis was born in Spain and has taught Spanish to adults in London

Dr John Baldwin is Lecturer in Phonetics at University College, London

Other titles in the series

Travellers' Spanish

D. L. Ellis, R. Ellis

Pronunciation **Dr J. Baldwin**

Pan Books London and Sydney

The publishers would like to thank the
Spanish National Tourist office for their help
during the preparation of this book

First published 1981 by Pan Books Ltd,
Cavaye Place, London SW10 9PG
© D. L. Ellis and R. Ellis 1981
ISBN 0 330 26294 7
Printed and bound in Great Britain by
Hunt Barnard Printing Ltd., Aylesbury, Bucks

Contents

6/Contents

Using the phrase book

- This phrase book is designed to help you get by in Spain, to get what you want or need. It concentrates on the simplest but most effective way you can express these needs in an unfamiliar language.
- The CONTENTS on p. 5 gives you a good idea of which section to consult for the phrase you need.
- The INDEX on p. 155 gives more detailed information about where to look for your phrase.
- When you have found the right page you will be given:
  - either – the exact phrase
  - or – help in making up a suitable sentence
  - and – help to get the pronunciation right
- The English sentences in **bold type** will be useful for you in a variety of different situations, so they are worth learning by heart. (See also DO IT YOURSELF, p. 146.)
- Wherever possible you will find help in understanding what Spanish people say to *you*, in reply to your questions.
- If you want to practise the basic nuts and bolts of the language further, look at the DO IT YOURSELF section starting on p. 146.
- Note especially these three sections:
  - Everyday expressions p. 11
  - Shop talk p. 54
  - Public notices p. 125
  - You are sure to want to refer to them most frequently.
- When you arrive in Spain make good use of the tourist information offices (see p. 23)
  - UK address:

    The Spanish National Tourist Office
    57 St James's Street, London SW1

A note on the pronunciation system

It is usual in phrase books for there to be a pronunciation section which tries to teach English-speaking tourists how to pronounce correctly the language of the country they are visiting. Such attempts are based on the argument that correct pronunciation is essential for comprehension. The system in this book, however, is founded on three quite different assumptions: firstly, that it is not possible to describe in print the sounds of a foreign language in such a way that the English speaker with no phonetic training will produce them accurately, or even intelligibly; secondly, that perfect pronunciation is not essential for communication, and lastly that the average visitor abroad is more interested in achieving successful communication than in learning how to pronounce new speech sounds. Observation and experience have shown these assumptions to be justified. The most important characteristic of the present system, therefore, is that it makes no attempt whatsoever to teach the sounds of the other language, but uses instead the nearest English sounds to them. The sentences transcribed for pronunciation are designed to be read as naturally as possible, as if they were ordinary English (of a generally south-eastern variety), and with no attempt to make the words sound 'foreign'. In this way you will still sound quite English, but you will at the same time be understood. Practice always helps performance, and it is a good idea to rehearse aloud any of the sentences you know you are going to need. When you do come to the point of using them, say them with conviction.

In Spanish it is important to stress or emphasize the syllables in italics, just as you would if we were to take as an English example: *li*ttle Jack *Hor*ner *sat* in the *cor*ner. Here we have ten syllables but only four stresses.

Of course you may enjoy trying to pronounce a foreign language as well as possible and the present system is a good way to start. However, since it uses only the sounds of English, you will very soon need to depart from it as you imitate the sounds you hear the native speaker produce and begin to relate them to the spelling of the other language. Spanish will pose no problems as there is an obvious and consistent relationship between pronunciation and spelling.
¡Suerte!

John Baldwin, 1980

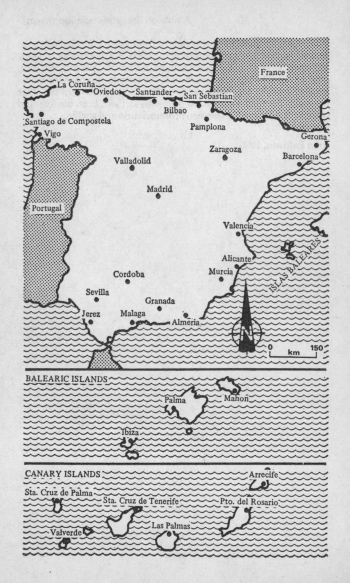

Everyday expressions

[See also 'Shop Talk', p. 54]

Hello	**Hola**
	o-la
Good morning	**Buenos días**
	bwen-os deeas
Good afternoon	**Buenas tardes**
	bwen-as tard-es
Goodnight	**Buenas noches**
	bwen-as noch-es
Good-bye	**Adiós**
	ad-yos
See you later	**Hasta luego**
	asta lweg-o
Yes	**Sí**
	see
Please	**Por favor**
	por fab-or
Yes, please	**Sí, por favor**
	see por fab-or
Great!	**¡Estupendo!**
	estoopendo
Thank you	**Gracias**
	grath-yas
Thank you very much	**Muchas gracias**
	moochas grath-yas
That's right	**Exacto**
	exacto
No	**No**
	no
No, thank you	**No, gracias**
	no grath-yas
I disagree	**No estoy de acuerdo**
	no estoy deh acwairdo
Excuse me ⎤	**Perdone**
Sorry	pairdon-eh
Don't mention it ⎤	**De nada**
That's OK	deh na-da

That's good ⎤ I like it ⎦	**Está bien** esta bee-en
That's no good ⎤ I don't like it ⎦	**No está bien** no esta bee-en
I know	**Ya sé** ya seh
I don't know	**No sé** no seh
It doesn't matter	**No importa** no importa
Where's the toilet, please?	**¿Dónde están los servicios, por favor?** dondeh estan los sairbith-yos por fab-or
How much is that? [*point*]	**¿Cuánto es?** cwanto es
Is the service included?	**¿Está incluido el servicio?** esta incloo-eedo el sairbith-yo
Do you speak English?	**¿Habla usted inglés?** abla oosted in-gles
I'm sorry ...	**Lo siento ...** lo see-ento ...
I don't speak Spanish	**no hablo español** no ablo espan-yol
I only speak a little Spanish	**sólo hablo un poco de español** sol-o ablo oon poco deh espan-yol
I don't understand	**no comprendo** no comprendo
Please can you ...	**Por favor, ¿puede ...** por fab-or pwed-eh ...
repeat that?	**repetir eso?** rep-eteer es-o
speak more slowly?	**hablar mas despacio?** ablar mas des-path-yo
write it down?	**escribirlo?** escrib-eerlo
What is this called in Spanish? [*point*]	**¿Cómo se llama esto en español?** com-o seh yama esto en espan-yol

Crossing the border

ESSENTIAL INFORMATION

- Don't waste time just before you leave rehearsing what you're going to say to the border officials – the chances are that you won't have to say anything at all, especially if you travel by air.
- It's more useful to check that you have your documents handy for the journey: passport, tickets, money, travellers' cheques, insurance documents, driving licence and car registration documents.
- Look out for these signs:
  ADUANA (customs)
  FRONTERA (border)
  FUNCIONARIOS DE ADUANAS (frontier police)
  CONTROL DE EQUIPAJES (baggage control)
  [For further signs and notices, see p. 125]
- You may be asked routine questions by the customs officials *[see below]*. If you have to give personal details see 'Meeting people', p. 14. The other important answer to know is 'Nothing': **Nada** (na-da)

ROUTINE QUESTIONS

Passport?	**¿Pasaporte?**
	pas-aporteh
Insurance?	**¿Seguro?**
	segoo-ro
Registration document? (logbook)	**¿Cartilla de propriedad?**
	cartee-ya deh prop-yed-ad
Ticket, please	**Billete, por favor**
	bee-yet-eh por fab-or
Have you anything to declare?	**¿Tiene algo que declarar?**
	tee-en-eh algo keh decla-rar
Where are you going?	**¿A dónde va usted?**
	ah dondeh ba oosted
How long are you staying?	**¿Cuánto tiempo va a quedarse?**
	cwanto tee-empo ba ah ked-ar-seh
Where have you come from?	**¿De dónde viene usted?**
	deh dondeh bee-eneh oosted

You may also have to fill in forms which ask for:

surname	**apellido**
first name	**nombre**
maiden name	**nombre de soltera**
place of birth	**lugar de nacimiento**
date of birth	**fecha de nacimiento**
address	**dirección**
nationality	**nacionalidad**
profession	**profesión**
passport number	**número de pasaporte**
issued at	**expedido en**
signature	**firma**

Meeting people

[See also 'Everyday expressions', p. 11]

Breaking the ice

Hello	**Hola**
	o-la
Good morning	**Buenos días**
	bwen-os de*e*as
How are you?	**¿Cómo está usted?**
	com-o est*a* oost*e*d
Pleased to meet you	**Mucho gusto**
	m*oo*cho g*oo*sto
I am here ...	**Estoy aquí ...**
	estoy ak-*ee* ...
on holiday	**de vacaciones**
	deh bakath-y*on*-es
on business	**de negocios**
	deh neg*o*th-yos
Can I offer you ...	**¿Puedo ofrecerle ...**
	pwed-o ofreth*air*-leh ...
a drink?	**una bebida?**
	*oo*na beb-*ee*da

a cigarette?	**un cigarrillo?**
	oon thiggar*ee*-yo
a cigar?	**un puro?**
	oon p*oo*-ro
Are you staying long?	**¿Va a quedarse mucho tiempo?**
	b*a* ah ked-*a*r-seh m*oo*cho tee-*e*mpo

Name

What is your name?	**¿Cómo se llama?**
	com-o seh y*a*ma
My name is ...	**Me llamo ...**
	meh y*a*mo ...

Family

Are you married?	**¿Es usted casado/a?***
	*e*s oosted cas*a*d-o/-ah
I am ...	**Soy ...**
	s*o*y ...
married	**casado/a***
	cas*a*d-o/-ah
single	**soltero/a***
	solt*a*ir*o*/-ah
This is ...	**Le presento a ...**
	leh pres-*e*nto ah
my wife	**mi esposa**
	mee espos-ah
my husband	**mi marido**
	mee ma-r*ee*do
my son	**mi hijo**
	mee *ee*ho
my daughter	**mi hija**
	mee *ee*h*a*
my (boy) friend	**mi novio**
	mee n*o*b-yo
my (girl) friend	**mi novia**
	mee n*o*b-ya
my (male/female) colleague	**mi colega**
	mee col-*e*g-ah
Do you have any children?	**¿Tiene hijos?**
	tee-en-*e*h *ee*hos

*For men use 'o', for women 'a'

I have ...	**Tengo ...**
	tengo ...
one daughter	**una hija**
	*oo*na *ee*ha
one son	**un hijo**
	oon *ee*ho
two daughters	**dos hijas**
	dos *ee*has
three sons	**tres hijos**
	tres *ee*hos
No, I haven't any children	**No, no tengo hijos**
	no no tengo *ee*hos

Where you live

Are you ...	**¿Es usted ...**
	es oosted ...
Spanish?	**español/a?**
	espan-yol/ah
South American?	**sudamericano/a?**
	soodameric*a*no/ah
I am ...	**Soy ...**
	soy ...
American	**americano/a**
	americ*a*no/ah
English	**inglés/a**
	in-gles/ah

[*For other nationalities, see p. 138*]

Where are you from?

I live ...	**Vivo ...**
	b*ee*-bo ...
in London	**en Londres**
	en londres
in England	**en Inglaterra**
	en ingla-t*e*rra
in the north	**en el norte**
	en el norteh
in the south	**en el sur**
	en el soor
in the east	**en el este**
	en el esteh

in the west	**en el oeste**
	en el o-esteh
in the centre	**en el centro**
	en el thentro

[*For other countries, see p. 138*]

For the businessman and woman

I'm from ... (firm's name)	**Soy de ...**
	soy deh ...
I have an appointment with ...	**Tengo una cita con ...**
	tengo oona theeta con ...
May I speak to ...?	**¿Puedo hablar con ...?**
	pwed-o ablar con ...
This is my card	**Esta es mi tarjeta**
	esta es mee tar-het-ah
I'm sorry I'm late	**Siento llegar tarde**
	see-ento yeg-ar tardeh
Can I fix another appointment?	**¿Puedo fijar otra cita?**
	pwed-o fee-har ot-ra theeta
I'm staying at the hotel (Madrid)	**Estoy en el hotel (Madrid)**
	estoy en el ot-el (madrid)
I'm staying in (St John's) road	**Estoy en la calle (San Juan)**
	estoy en la ca-yeh (san hwan)

Asking the way

ESSENTIAL INFORMATION

- Keep a look out for all these place names as you will find them on shops, maps and notices.

WHAT TO SAY

| Excuse me, please | **Perdone, por favor** |
| | pairdon-eh por fab-or |

How do I get ...
      ¿Para ir ...
      p*a*ra *ee*r ...

  to Madrid?
      a Madrid?
      ah mad*ree*d

  to calle Alfonso Primero?
      a la calle Alfonso Primero?
      ah la c*a*-yeh alf*o*nso prim-*ai*ro

  to the Hotel Castilla?
      al hotel Castilla?
      al ot-*e*l cast*ee*-ya

  to the airport?
      al aeropuerto?
      al airo-pw*air*to

  to the beach?
      a la playa?
      ah la pl*a*-ya

  to the bus station?
      a la estación de autobuses?
      ah la estath-y*o*n deh
        ah-ooto-b*oo*ses

  to the historic site?
      a la ciudad antigua?
      ah la thee-ood*a*d ant*i*gwa

  to the market?
      al mercado?
      al mairc*a*d-o

  to the police station?
      a la comisaría de policía?
      ah la comisar*ee*a deh polith*ee*a

  to the port?
      al puerto?
      al pw*air*to

  to the post office?
      a correos?
      ah cor-r*e*h-os

  to the railway station?
      a la estación de tren?
      ah la estath-y*o*n deh tren

  to the sports stadium?
      al estadio de deportes?
      al est*a*d-yo deh dep-*o*rt-es

  to the tourist information
     office?
      a la oficina de información y
        turismo?
      ah la ofith*ee*na deh informath-y*o*n
        ee too-r*i*smo

  to the town centre?
      al centro de la ciudad?
      al th*e*ntro deh la thee-ood*a*d

  to the town hall?
      al ayuntamiento?
      al a-yoontam-y*e*nto

Excuse me, please
      Perdone, por favor
      paird*o*n-eh por fab-*o*r

Is there ... near by?
      ¿Hay ... cerca?
      *a*h-ee ... th*ai*rca

  an art gallery
      una galería de arte
      *oo*na gal-er*ee*a deh *a*rteh

a baker's	**una panadería**
	*oo*na panad-er*ee*ah
a bank	**un banco**
	oon banco
a bar	**un bar**
	oon bar
a botanical garden	**un jardín botánico**
	oon hard*ee*n botanic-o
a bus stop	**una parada de autobús**
	*oo*na parad-ah deh ah-ooto-boos
a butcher's	**una carnicería**
	*oo*na carnith-cr*ee*a
a café	**una cafetería**
	*oo*na cafet-er*ee*a
a cake shop	**una pastelería**
	*oo*na pastel-er*ee*a
a campsite	**un camping**
	oon camping
a car park	**un aparcamiento**
	oon aparcam-yento
a change bureau	**una oficina de cambio**
	*oo*na ofith*ee*na deh cumb-yo
a chemist's	**una farmacia**
	*oo*na farmath-ya
a church	**una iglesia**
	*oo*na cegles-ya
a cinema	**un cine**
	oon thin-eh
a delicatessen	**una mantequería**
	*oo*na mantek-er*ee*a
a dentist's	**un dentista**
	oon dentista
a department store	**unos almacenes**
	*oo*nos almath-en-es
a disco	**una discoteca**
	oona discotec-ah
a doctor's surgery	**un consultorio médico**
	oon consooltorio medic-o
a dry cleaner's	**una tintorería**
	*oo*na tintor-er*ee*a
a fishmonger's	**una pescadería**
	*oo*na pescad-er*ee*a

Is there . . . near by? **¿Hay . . . cerca?**
ah-ee . . . thairca

a garage (for repairs) **un garaje**
oon ga-raheh

a greengrocer's **una verdulería**
oona berdool-ereea

a grocer's **una tienda de comestibles**
oona tee-enda deh com-estee-bles

a hairdresser's **una peluquería**
oona pelook-ereea

a hardware shop **una ferretería**
oona ferret-ereea

a Health and Social **una oficina de la Seguridad**
Security Office **Social**
*oona ofitheena deh la
segoo-reedad soth-yal*

a hospital **un hospital**
oon ospital

a hotel **un hotel**
oon ot-el

an ice-cream parlour **una heladería**
oona ellad-ereea

a laundry **una lavandería**
oona laband-ereea

a museum **un museo**
oon moo-sey-o

a newsagent's **una tienda de periódicos**
oona tee-enda deh peri-odicos

a nightclub **una sala de fiestas**
oona sal-ah deh fee-estas

a park **un parque**
oon parkeh

a petrol station **una gasolinera**
oona gasolin-erra

a post box **un buzón**
oon boothon

a public garden **un jardín público**
oon hardeen pooblico

a public toilet **unos servicios públicos**
oonos sairbith-yos pooblicos

a restaurant **un restaurante**
oon resta-ooranteh

a snack bar	**un bar**
	oon b*a*r
a sports ground	**un campo de deportes**
	oon c*a*mpo dch dep-*o*rt-es
a supermarket	**un supermercado**
	oon supermairc*a*d-o
a sweet shop	**una bombonería**
	*oo*na bombon-er*ee*a
a swimming pool	**una piscina**
	oona pis-th*ee*na
a taxi stand	**una parada de taxis**
	*oo*na par*a*d-ah deh t*a*xis
a telephone	**un teléfono**
	oon tel*e*f-ono
a theatre	**un teatro**
	oon teh-*a*tro
a tobacconist's	**un estanco**
	oon est*a*nco
a travel agent's	**una agencia de viajes**
	*oo*na ahenth-ya deh bee-*ah*-hes
a youth hostel	**un albergue juvenil**
	oon alb*a*ir-gch hooben-*ee*l
a zoo	**un zoo**
	oon th*o*h-o

DIRECTIONS

- Asking where a place is, or if a place is near by, is one thing; making sense of the answer is another.
- Here are some of the most important key directions and replies.

Left	**Izquierda**
	ithk-y*ai*rda
Right	**Derecha**
	der*e*ch-ah
Straight on	**Todo recto**
	t*o*do r*e*cto
There	**Allí**
	ay*ee*

First left/right	**La primera a la izquierda/derecha**
	la prim-*ai*ra ah la ithk-y*air*da/ derech-a
Second left/right	**La segunda a la izquiera/derecha**
	la seg-*oo*nda ah la ithk-y*air*da/ derech-a
At the crossroads	**En el cruce**
	en el cr*oo*theh
At the traffic lights	**En el semáforo**
	en el sem*a*foro
At the roundabout	**En el cruce giratorio**
	en el cr*oo*theh gee-rator*ee*-o
At the level crossing	**En el paso a nivel**
	en el p*a*s-o ah nib-*e*l
It's near/far	**Está cerca/lejos**
	esta th*air*ca/l*e*h-hos
One kilometre	**A un kilómetro**
	ah oon kil*o*metro
Two kilometres	**A dos kilómetros**
	ah dos kil*o*metros
Five minutes ...	**A cinco minutos ...**
	ah th*i*n-co min*oo*tos ...
on foot	**a pie**
	ah pee-*eh*
by car	**en coche**
	en c*o*ch-eh
Take ...	**Tome ...**
	t*o*m-eh ...
the bus	**el autobús**
	el ah-ooto-b*oo*s
the train	**el tren**
	el tren
the tram	**el tranvía**
	el tramb*ee*a
the underground	**el metro**
	el m*e*tro

[*For public transport, see p. 116*]

The tourist information office

ESSENTIAL INFORMATION

- Most towns and even some villages in Spain have a tourist information office.
- Look for these words:
  OFICINA DE INFORMACION Y TURISMO
  DELEGACION PROVINCIAL DE INFORMACION Y TURISMO
  OFICINA MUNICIPAL DE INFORMACION
- Sometimes there may be signposts with these abbreviations: **MIT (Ministerio de Información y Turismo)** and **CITE (Centro de Iniciativas Turísticas Españolas)**.
- These offices provide free information in the form of printed leaflets, fold-outs, brochures, lists and plans.
- You may have to pay for some types of document but this is not usual.
- For finding a tourist office, see p. 17.

WHAT TO SAY

Please, have you got ...	**Por favor, ¿tiene ...** por fa-bor tee-en-eh ...
a plan of the town?	**un plano de la ciudad?** oon plan-o deh la thee-oodad
a list of hotels?	**una lista de hoteles?** oona leesta deh ot-el-es
a list of campsites?	**una lista de campings?** oona leesta de campings
a list of restaurants	**una lista de restaurantes?** oona leesta deh resta-oorant-es
a list of coach excursions?	**una lista de excursiones en autobús?** oona leesta deh excoors-yon-es en ah-ooto-boos
a leaflet on the town?	**un folleto de la ciudad?** oon foyeto deh la thee-oodad
a leaflet on the region?	**un folleto de la región?** oon foyeto deh la reh-hee-on

Please, have you got ...	**Por favor, ¿tiene ...** por fa-bor tee-en-eh ...
a railway timetable?	**un horario de trenes?** oon orarrio deh tren-es
a bus timetable?	**un horario de autobuses?** oon orarrio deh ah-ooto-boos-es
In English, please	**En inglés, por favor** en in-gles por fab-or
How much do I owe you?	**¿Cuánto le debo?** cwanto leh deb-o
Can you recommend ...	**¿Puede recomendarme ...** pwed-eh recommendar-meh ...
a cheap hotel?	**un hotel barato?** oon ot-el ba-rat-o
a cheap restaurant?	**un restaurante barato?** oon resta-ooranteh ba-rat-o
Can you make a booking for me?	**¿Puede hacerme una reserva?** pwed-eh athair-meh oona res-airba

LIKELY ANSWERS

You need to understand when the answer is 'No'. You should be able to tell by the assistant's facial expression, tone of voice and gesture, but there are some language clues, such as:

No	**No** no
I'm sorry	**Lo siento** lo see-ento
I don't have a list of campsites	**No tengo una lista de campings** no tengo oona leesta deh campings
I haven't got any left	**No me queda ninguno** no meh ked-ah nin-goono
It's free	**Es gratis** es grat-is

Accommodation

Hotel

ESSENTIAL INFORMATION

- If you want hotel-type accommodation, all the following words in capital letters are worth looking for on name boards:
  HOTEL (accommodation with all facilities, the quality depending on the star rating)
  HOTEL-RESIDENCIA (similar to the above but often for longer stays)
  PENSION (small, privately run hotel)
  HOSTAL
  FONDA (a modest form of **pensión**)
  MOTEL
  ALBERGUE (often picturesque type of hotel situated in the countryside)
  PARADOR (converted palaces and castles in recognized beauty spots – relatively expensive)
- The last two are run by the **Secretaria de Estado de Turismo** (Secretary of State for Tourism).
- In some places, you will find the following: **CAMAS** (beds), **HABITACIONES** (rooms), **CASA** (house) followed by the owner's name or **CASA DE HUESPEDES** (guest house) – these are all alternatives to a **pensión**.
- Hotels are divided into five classes (from luxury to tourist class and **pensiones** into three.
- A list of hotels and **pensiones** in the town or district can usually be obtained at the local tourist information office [see p. 23]
- The cost is displayed in the room itself, so you can check it when having a look around before agreeing to stay.
- The displayed cost is for the room itself, per night and not per person. Breakfast is extra and therefore optional.
- Service and VAT is always included in the cost of the room, so tipping is voluntary. In Spain, however, it is normal practice to tip porters and waiters.

- Not all hotels provide meals, apart from breakfast. A **pensión** always provides meals. Breakfast is continental style: coffee/tea with rolls and jam.
- When registering you will be asked to leave your passport at the reception desk and to complete a form.
- Finding a hotel, see p. 17.

WHAT TO SAY

I have a booking	**Tengo una reserva**
	tengo _oo_na res-_air_ba
Have you any vacancies, please?	**¿Tiene habitaciones libres, por favor?**
	tee-en-eh abeetath-yon-es _lee_-bres por fab-_or_
Can I book a room?	**¿Puedo reservar una habitación?**
	pwed-o res-airb_ar_ _oo_na abeetath-y_on_
It's for ...	**Es para ...**
	es para ...
one person	**una persona**
	_oo_na pairson-ah
two people	**dos personas**
	dos pairson-as

[_For numbers, see p. 131_]

It's for ...	**Es para ...**
	es para ...
one night	**una noche**
	_oo_na noch-eh
two nights	**dos noches**
	dos noch-es
one week	**una semana**
	_oo_na sem-_a_nna
two weeks	**dos semanas**
	dos sem-_a_nnas
I would like ...	**Quiero ...**
	kee-_airo_ ...
a room	**una habitación**
	_oo_na abeetath-yon

two rooms	**dos habitaciones**
	dos abeetath-yon-es
with a single bed	**con una cama individual**
	con oona cam-ah indibid-wal
with two single beds	**con dos camas individuales**
	con dos cam-as indibid-wal-es
with a double bed	**con una cama doble**
	con oona cam-ah dobleh
with a toilet	**con servicio**
	con sairbith-yo
with a bathroom	**con baño**
	con ban-yo
with a shower	**con ducha**
	con doocha
with a cot	**con una cuna**
	con oona coona
with a balcony	**con balcón**
	con balcon
I would like ...	**Quiero ...**
	kee-airo ...
full board	**pensión completa**
	pens-yon complet-ah
half board	**media pensión**
	med-ya pens-yon
bed and breakfast	**desayuno incluido**
	desa-yoono incloo-eedo
[See Essential information]	
Do you serve meals?	**¿Sirven comidas?**
	seerben com-eedas
At what time is ...	**¿A qué hora es ...**
	ah keh ora es ...
breakfast?	**el desayuno?**
	el desa-yoono
lunch?	**la comida?**
	la com-eeda
dinner?	**la cena?**
	la then-ah
How much is it?	**¿Cuánto es?**
	cwanto es
Can I look at the room?	**¿Puedo ver la habitación?**
	pwed-o bair la abeetath-yon

I'd prefer a room ...
Prefiero una habitación ...
pref-y*air*-o *oo*na abeetath-y*o*n ...

  at the front/at the back
exterior/interior
exterri-*or*/ interri-*or*

OK, I'll take it
Está bien, la tomo
est*a* bee-*e*n la t*o*m-o

No thanks, I won't take it
No gracias, no la tomo
no gr*a*th-yas no la t*o*m-o

The key to number (10), please
La llave de la número (diez), por favor
la y*a*b-eh deh la n*oo*mairo (dee-*e*th) por fab-*o*r

Please, may I have ...
Por favor, ¿puede darme ...
por fab-*or* pwed-eh d*a*rmeh ...

  a coat hanger?
una percha?
*oo*na p*ai*rcha

  a towel?
una toalla?
*oo*na toh-*a*l-ya

  a glass?
un vaso?
oon b*a*sso

  some soap?
jabón?
hab-*o*n

  an ashtray?
un cenicero?
oon thenee-th*ai*r-o

  another pillow?
otra almohada?
*o*t-ra almo-*a*d-ah

  another blanket?
otra manta?
*o*t-ra m*a*nta

Come in!
¡Adelante!
ad-el-*a*nteh

One moment, please!
¡Un momento, por favor!
oon mom*e*nto por fab-*o*r

Please can you ...
Por favor, ¿puede ...
por fab-*or* pw*e*d-eh ...

  do this laundry/dry cleaning?
lavar esto/limpiar esto en seco?
lab-*ar* esto/limp-y*ar* esto en s*e*c-o

  call me at ... ?
llamarme a ... ?
ya-m*a*rmeh ah ...

  help me with my luggage?
ayudarme con el equipaje?
a-yood*a*rmeh con el ekeep*a*-heh

  call me a taxi for ... ?
llamarme un taxi para ... ?
ya-m*a*rmeh oon taxi p*a*ra ...

[*For times, see p. 133*]

The bill, please

La cuenta, por favor
la cwenta por fab-or

Is service included?

¿Está incluido el servicio?
esta incloo-eedo el sairbith-yo

I think this is wrong

Creo que esto está mal
creh-o keh esto esta mal

Can you give me a receipt?

¿Puede darme un recibo?
pwed-eh darmeh oon retheebo

At breakfast

Some more . . . , please

Mas . . . , por favor
mas . . . por fab-or

coffee

café
cafeh

tea

té
teh

bread

pan
pan

butter

mantequilla
mantehkee-ya

jam

mermclada
mairmel-ad-ah

May I have a boiled egg?

¿Puedo haber un huevo pasado por agua?
pwed-o abair oon web-o pasad-o por agwa

LIKELY REACTIONS

Have you an identity document, please?

¿Tiene usted un documento de identidad, por favor?
tee-en-eh oosted oon docoomento deh id-entidad por fab-or

What's your name? [see p. 14]

¿Cómo se llama?
com-o seh yama

Sorry, we're full

Lo siento, está lleno
lo see-ento esta yen-o

I haven't any rooms left

No me quedan habitaciones
no meh ked-an abeetath-yon-es

Do you want to have a look?

¿Quiere ver la habitación?
kee-aireh bair la abeetath-yon

How many people is it for?	**¿Para cuántas personas es?**
	para cwantas pairson-as es
From (seven o'clock) onwards	**Desde (las siete) en adelante**
	desdeh (las see-et-eh) en
	ad-el-anteh
From (midday) onwards	**Desde (mediodía) en adelante**
	desdeh (med-yo deea) en
[For times, see p. 133]	ad-el-anteh
It's (1000) pesetas	**Son (mil) pesetas**
[For numbers, see p. 131]	son (mil) pes-et-as

Camping and youth hostelling

ESSENTIAL INFORMATION

Camping
- Look for the word: **CAMPING**
- Be prepared to have to pay:
  per person
  for the car (if applicable)
  for the tent or caravan plot
  for electricity
  for hot showers
- You must provide proof of identity such as your passport.
- In Spain, most campsites are situated along the coast and those inland are few and far between. You can camp off-site with the permission of the authorities and/or the landowner; however, there are a number of regulations governing where you can or cannot camp – the Spanish Tourist Office in London has details so check with them before travelling abroad.
- Camping carnets are no longer essential but advisable as they do provide third-party insurance for those camping off-site.
- During the high season it is advisable to book in advance by writing direct to the campsite.
- Persons under the age of sixteen are not admitted on a site unless accompanied by an adult.

Youth hostels

- Look for the words: **ALBERGUE JUVENIL**.
- You will be asked for a YHA card and passport on arrival.
- Food and cooking facilities vary from hostel to hostel and you may have to help with the domestic chores.
- You must take your own sleeping bag lining but bedding can sometimes be hired on arrival.
- In the high season it is advisable to book beds in advance, and your stay will be limited to a maximum of three consecutive nights per hostel.
- Apply to the Spanish Tourist office in London or local tourist offices in Spain [see p. 23] for lists of youth hostels and details of regulations for hostellers.
- For buying or replacing camping equipment, see p. 52.

WHAT TO SAY

I have a booking	**Tengo una reserva**
	tengo oona res-airba
Have you any vacancies?	**¿Tiene plazas libres?**
	tee-en-eh plathas lee-bres
It's for ...	**Es para ...**
	es para ...
one adult/one person	**un adulto/una persona**
	oon adoolto/oona pairson-ah
two adults/two people	**dos adultos/dos personas**
	dos adooltos/dos pairson-as
and one child	**y un niño**
	ee oon neen-yo
and two children	**y dos niños**
	ee dos neen-yos
It's for ...	**Es para ...**
	es para ...
one night	**una noche**
	oona noch-eh
two nights	**dos noches**
	dos noch-es
one week	**una semana**
	oona sem-anna
two weeks	**dos semanas**
	dos sem-annas

How much is it ...	**¿Cuánto es ...**
	cwanto es ...
for the tent?	**por la tienda?**
	por la tee-enda
for the caravan?	**por la caravana?**
	por la caraban-ah
for the car?	**por el coche?**
	por el coch-eh
for the electricity?	**por la electricidad**
	por la electrithee-dad
per person?	**por persona?**
	por pairson-ah
per day/night?	**por día/noche?**
	por deea/noch-eh
May I look round?	**¿Puedo mirar?**
	pwed-o mee-rar
Do you close the gate/door at night?	**¿Cierran la puerta por la noche?**
	thee-erran la pwairta por la noch-eh
Do you provide anything ...	**¿Dan ustedes algo ...**
	dan oosted-es algo ...
to eat?	**de comer?**
	deh com-air
to drink?	**de beber?**
	deh beb-air
Is there/are there ...	**¿Hay ...**
	ah-ee ...
a bar?	**bar?**
	bar
hot showers?	**duchas calientes?**
	doochas cal-yentes
a kitchen?	**cocina?**
	cotheena
a laundry?	**lavandería?**
	laband-ereea
a restaurant?	**restaurante?**
	resta-ooranteh
a shop?	**tienda?**
	tee-enda
a swimming pool?	**piscina?**
	pis-theena

a takeaway? | **tienda de comidas preparadas?**
[*For food shopping, see p. 59,* | tee-enda deh com-*ee*das
and for eating and drinking | prepa-*rad*-as
out, see p. 80]

I would like a counter for the shower | **Quiero una ficha para la ducha**
 | kee-*airo oo*na f*ee*cha para la d*oo*cha

Where are ... | **¿Dónde están ...**
 | dondeh estan ...

the dustbins? | **los cubos de basura?**
 | los c*oo*bos deh bas*oo*-ra

the showers? | **las duchas?**
 | las d*oo*chas

the toilets? | **los servicios?**
 | los sairb*ith* yos

At what time must one ... | **¿A qué hora debe uno ...**
 | ah keh *o*ra d*eb*-eh *oo*no ...

go to bed? | **acostarse?**
 | acost*ar*-seh

get up? | **levantarse?**
 | leb-ant*ar*-seh

Please, have you got ... | **Por favor, ¿tiene ...**
 | por fab-*or* tee-*en*-eh ...

a broom? | **una escoba?**
 | *oo*na escob-ah

a corkscrew? | **un sacacorchos?**
 | *oo*n sac-ac*orc*hos

a drying-up cloth? | **un paño de cocina?**
 | *oo*n pan-yo deh coth*ee*na

a fork? | **un tenedor?**
 | *oo*n ten-ed-*or*

a fridge? | **un frigorífico?**
 | oon frig-or*i*fico

a frying pan? | **una sartén?**
 | *oo*na sarten

an iron? | **una plancha?**
 | *oo*na plancha

a knife? | **un cuchillo?**
 | oon cooch*ee*-yo

a plate? | **un plato?**
 | oon plat-o

Please, have you got ...	**Por favor, ¿tiene ...**
	por fab-or tee-*en*-eh ...
a saucepan?	**una cacerola?**
	*oo*na catheh-r*o*l-ah
a teaspoon?	**una cucharilla?**
	*oo*na coochar*ee*-ya
a tin opener?	**un abrelatas?**
	*oo*n abrel-*at*-as
any washing powder?	**detergente?**
	det-air-h*e*nteh
any washing-up liquid?	**lavavajillas?**
	lababa-h*ee*-yas
The bill, please	**La cuenta, por favor**
	la c*we*nta por fab-*or*

Problems

The toilet	**El servicio**
	el sairb*i*th-yo
The shower	**La ducha**
	la d*oo*cha
The tap	**El grifo**
	el gr*ee*fo
The razor point	**El enchufe de la maquinilla de afeitar**
	el ench*oo*feh deh la makin*ee*-ya deh aff*ay*t*a*r
The light	**La luz**
	la l*oo*th
... is not working	**... está roto/a**
	... est*a* r*o*t-o/ah
My camping gas has run out	**Mi camping gas se ha acabado**
	mee c*a*mping g*a*s seh *a*h acab*a*d-o

LIKELY REACTIONS

Have you an identity document?
¿Tiene usted un documento de identidad?
tee-*en*-eh oost*ed* oon docoomento deh id-entid*ad*

Your membership card, please
Su carnet, por favor
soo carnet por fab-*or*

What's your name? [see p. 14]
¿Cómo se llama?
com-o seh y*a*ma

Sorry, we're full
Lo siento, está lleno
lo see-ento est*a* yen-o

How many people is it for?
¿Para cuántas personas es?
p*a*ra cw*a*ntas pairson-as *es*

How many nights is it for?
¿Para cuántas noches es?
p*a*ra cw*a*ntas noch-es *es*

It's (100) pesetas . . .
Son (cien) pesetas . . .
son (thee-*en*) pes-*et*-as . . .

per day/per night
por día/por noche
por d*ee*a/por noch-eh

[*For numbers, see p. 131*]

Rented accommodation: problem solving

ESSENTIAL INFORMATION

- If you're looking for accommodation to rent, look out for:
  SE ALQUILA (to let)
  PISO (flat)
  APARTAMENTO (flat)
  VILLA (villa)
  CHALET (chalet)
  CASA DE CAMPO (cottage)
  FINCA (country house)
- For arranging details of your let, see 'Hotel' p. 25.
- Key words you will meet if renting on the spot:
  la fianza (deposit)   **la llave** (key)
  la fee-*a*ntha   la y*a*b-eh
- Having arranged your own accommodation and arrived with
  the key, check the obvious basics that you take for granted
  at home.
  Electricity Voltage? Razors and small appliances brought
  from home may need adjusting. You may need an adaptor.
  Gas Town gas or bottled gas? Butane gas must be kept in-
  doors, propane gas must be kept outdoors.
  Cooker Don't be surprised to find:
  the grill inside the oven, or no grill at all
  a lid covering the rings which lifts up to form a 'splash-
  back'
  a mixture of two gas rings and two electric rings.
  Toilet Mains drainage or septic tank? Don't flush disposable
  nappies or anything else down the toilet if you are on a septic
  tank.
  Water Find the stopcock. Check taps and plugs – they may
  not operate in the way you are used to. Check how to turn on
  (or light) the hot water.
  Windows Check the method of opening and closing windows
  and shutters.
  Insects Is an insecticide spray provided? If not, get one locally.
  Equipment For buying or replacing equipment, see p. 52.
- You will probably have an official agent, but be clear in
  your own mind who to contact in an emergency, even if it is
  only a neighbour in the first instance.

WHAT TO SAY

My name is ...	**Me llamo ...**
	meh yam-o ...
I'm staying at ...	**Estoy en ...**
	estoy en ...
They've cut off ...	**Han cortado ...**
	an cortad-o ...
the electricity	**la electricidad**
	la electrithee-dad
the gas	**el gas**
	el gas
the water	**el agua**
	el agwa
Is there ... in the area?	**¿Hay ... en el área?**
	ah-ee ... en el a-reh-a
an electrician	**un electricista**
	oon electri-thista
a plumber	**un fontanero**
	oon fontan-airo
a gas fitter	**un empleado del gas**
	oon empleh-ad-o del gas
Where is ...	**¿Dónde está ...**
	dondeh esta ...
the fuse box?	**la caja de fusibles**
	la ca-ha deh foosee-bles
the stopcock?	**la llave de paso?**
	la yab-eh deh pas-o
the boiler?	**la caldera?**
	la caldaira
the water heater?	**el calentador del agua?**
	el callenta-dor del agwa
Is there ...	**¿Hay ...**
	ah-ee ...
town gas?	**gas ciudad?**
	gas thee-oodad
bottled gas?	**gas en botella?**
	gas en botel-ya
a septic tank?	**cisterna?**
	thistairna
central heating?	**calefacción central?**
	callefak-thion thentral

The cooker	**La cocina**
	la coth*ee*na
The hair dryer	**El secador**
	el sec-a-d*o*r
The heating	**La calefacción**
	la callefak-thi*o*n
The immersion heater	**El calentador de immersión**
	el callenta-d*o*r deh inmairs-y*o*n
The iron	**La plancha**
	la pl*a*ncha
The pilot light	**La luz del piloto**
	la l*oo*th del pil-*o*t-o
The refrigerator	**El frigorífico**
	el frig-or*í*fico
The telephone	**El teléfono**
	el tel*e*f-ono
The toilet	**El servicio**
	el sairb*i*th-yo
The washing machine	**La lavadora**
	la lab-a-d*o*ra
... is not working	**... está roto/a**
	... est*a* r*o*t-o/-ah
Where can I get ...	**¿Dónde puedo obtener ...**
	d*o*ndeh pw*e*d-o obten-*air* ...
an adaptor for this?	**un adaptador para esto?**
	oon adapta-d*o*r p*a*ra *e*sto
a bottle of butane gas?	**una botella de gas butano?**
	*oo*na bot*e*l-ya deh g*a*s boot*a*n-o
a bottle of propane gas?	**una botella de gas propano?**
	*oo*na bot*e*l-ya deh g*a*s prop*a*n-o
a fuse?	**un fusible?**
	oon foos*ee*bleh
an insecticide spray?	**un insecticida en spray?**
	oon insecti-th*ee*da en spr*a*-ee
a light bulb?	**una bombilla?**
	*oo*na bomb*ee*-ya
The drain	**El desagüe**
	el des-*a*g-we
The toilet	**El servicio**
	el sairb*i*th-yo
... is blocked	**... está atascado**
	... est*a* at-asc*a*do
The sink is blocked	**La fregadera está atascada**
	la freg-ad*ai*ra est*a* at-asc*a*da

The gas is leaking	**Hay un escape de gas** *ah*-ee oon escap-eh deh g*as*
Can you mend it straightaway?	**¿Puede arreglarlo ahora mismo?** pwed-eh arregl*ar*-lo ah-*o*ra m*i*smo
When can you mend it?	**¿Cuándo puede arreglarlo?** cw*a*ndo pwed-eh arregl*a*r-lo
How much do I owe you?	**¿Cuánto le debo?** cw*a*nto leh d*e*b-o
When is the rubbish collected?	**¿Cuándo recogen la basura?** cw*a*ndo rec-*o*-hen la bas*oo*-ra

LIKELY REACTIONS

What's your name?	**¿Cómo se llama?** com-o seh y*a*ma
What's your address?	**¿Cuál es su dirección?** cw*a*l *e*s soo dirrek-thi*o*n
There's a shop . . .	**Hay una tienda . . .** *a*h-ee oona tee-*e*nda . . .
in town	**en la ciudad** en la thee-ood*a*d
in the village	**en el pueblo** en el pw*e*b-lo
I can't come . . .	**No puedo ir . . .** no pwed-o *ee*r . . .
today	**hoy** *o*y
this week	**esta semana** *e*sta sem-*u*nna
until Monday	**hasta el lunes** *a*sta el l*oo*n-es
I can come . . .	**Puedo ir . . .** pwed-o *ee*r . . .
on Tuesday	**el martes** el m*a*rt-es
when you want	**cuando usted quiera** cw*a*ndo oosted kee-*ai*ra
Every day	**Cada día** c*a*d-ah d*e*ea
Every other day	**Un día sin otro** oon d*e*ea sin *o*t-ro
On Wednesdays [*For days of the week, p. 135*]	**Los miércoles** los mee-*ai*rcol-es

General shopping

The chemist's

ESSENTIAL INFORMATION

- Look for the word
  FARMACIA (chemist's),
  or these signs.
- Medicines (drugs) are available
  only at a chemist's.
- Some non-drugs can be bought at a supermarket or department store, of course.
- Try the chemist *before* going to a doctor: they are usually qualified to treat minor injuries.
- Normal opening times are 9 a.m. – 1 p.m. and 4 p.m. – 8 p.m.
- If the chemist's is shut, a notice on the door headed **FARMACIAS DE GUARDIA** gives the address of the nearest chemist on duty.
- Some toiletries can also be bought at a **PERFUMERIA,** but they will probably be more expensive.
- Finding a chemist, see p. 17.

WHAT TO SAY

I'd like ...	Quiero ...
	kee-*airo* ...
some Alka Seltzer	**Alka Seltzer**
	alka selthair
some antiseptic	**antiséptico**
	antiseptico
some aspirin	**aspirinas**
	aspirin-as
some bandage	**vendas**
	bend-as
some cotton wool	**algodón**
	algod-on
some eye drops	**gotas para los ojos**
	got-as para los o-hos

I'd like . . .	**Quiero . . .**
	kee-*airo* . . .
some foot powder	**polvos para los pies**
	pol-bos para los pee-*es*
some gauze dressing	**gasa**
	gas-ah
some inhalant	**inhalante**
	in-a*lan*teh
some insect repellent	**loción contra los insectos**
	loth-*yon* contra los in*sectos*
some lip salve	**cacao para los labios**
	caca-o para los *lab*-yos
some nose drops	**gotas para la nariz**
	got-as para la nar*eeth*
some sticking plaster	**esparadrapo**
	esparad*rappo*
some throat pastilles	**pastillas para la garganta**
	past*ee*-yas para la gar*ganta*
some Vaseline	**Vaselina**
	bas-el-*eena*
I'd like something for . . .	**Quiero algo para . . .**
	Kee-*airo algo* para . . .
bites/stings	**las picaduras**
	las pic-ad*ooras*
burns	**las quemaduras**
	las kem-ad*ooras*
chilblains	**los sabañones**
	los sab-an-*yon*-es
a cold	**el catarro**
	el cat*arro*
constipation	**el estreñimiento**
	el estren-yee-mee-*ento*
a cough	**la tos**
	la *tos*
diarrhoea	**la diarrea**
	la dee-ah-*reh*-ah
ear-ache	**el dolor de oído**
	el dol-*or* deh o-*ee*do
flu	**la gripe**
	la *greep*-eh
scalds	**las escaldaduras**
	las escald-ad*ooras*

I'd like something for ...	Quiero algo para ...
	kee-*air*o *a*lgo p*a*ra ...
sore gums	**el dolor de encías**
	el dol-*or* deh enth*ee*-as
sprains	**las torceduras**
	las torthed-*oo*ras
sunburn	**las quemaduras de sol**
	las kem-ad*oo*ras deh sol
travel sickness	**el mareo**
	el ma-r*e*yo

I need ...	Necesito ...
	neth-es*ee*to ...
some baby food	**comida para niños**
	com-*ee*da p*a*ra n*ee*n-yos
some contraceptives	**anticonceptivos**
	anti-conthept-*ee*bos
some deodorant	**desodorante**
	desodor*a*nteh
some disposable nappies	**pañales de papel**
	pan-y*a*l-es deh pap-*e*l
some handcream	**crema para las manos**
	crem-ah p*a*ra las m*a*n-os
some lipstick	**lápiz de labios**
	l*a*p-ith deh l*a*b-yos
some make-up remover	**crema limpiadora**
	crem-ah limp-yad*o*ra
some paper tissues	**tisús**
	tis*oo*s
some razor blades	**cuchillas**
	cooch*ee*-yas
some safety pins	**imperdibles**
	impaird*ee*-bles
some sanitary towels	**compresas**
	compr*e*s-as
some shaving cream	**crema de afeitar**
	crem-ah deh afeyt*a*r
some soap	**jabón**
	hab-*o*n
some suntan lotion/oil	**loción/aceite bronceador**
	loth-y*o*n/ath*a*y-teh bronth*e*h-ad*o*r
some talcum powder	**polvos de talco**
	p*o*l-bos deh t*a*lco

some Tampax	**Tampax**
	t*a*mpax
some (soft) toilet paper	**papel higiénico (suave)**
	pap-*el* eehi-yennico (sw*a*-beh)
some toothpaste	**pasta de dientes**
	pasta deh dee-ent-es
[*For other essential*	

[*For other essential*
expressions, see 'Shop talk', p. 54]

Holiday items

ESSENTIAL INFORMATION

- Places to shop at and signs to look for:
  LIBRERIA-PAPELERIA (stationery)
  FOTOGRAFIA (films)
  MATERIAL FOTOGRAFICO (films)
  and the main department stores:
  GALERIAS PRECIADOS
  SEPU
  EL CORTE INGLES

WHAT TO SAY

Where can I buy ... ?	**¿Dónde puedo comprar ... ?**
	d*o*ndeh pw*e*d-o compr*a*r ...
I'd like ...	**Quiero ...**
	kee-*ai*ro ...
a bag	**un bolso**
	oon b*o*lso
a beach ball	**una pelota para la playa**
	*oo*na pel*o*ta p*a*ra la pl*a*-ya
a bucket	**un cubo**
	oon c*oo*bo
an English newspaper	**un periódico inglés**
	oon peri-*o*d-ico in-gl*e*s
some envelopes	**sobres**
	s*o*b-res

I'd like . . .	Quiero . . .
	kee-*airo* . . .
a guide book	**una guía**
	*oo*na gh*ee*a
a map (of the area)	**un plano (del área)**
	oon pl*a*n-o (del *a*-reh-a)
some postcards	**postales**
	post*a*l-es
a spade	**una pala**
	*oo*na p*a*l-ah
a straw hat	**un sombrero de paja**
	oon sombr*airo* deh p*a*-ha
a suitcase	**una maleta**
	*oo*na mal*e*t-ah
some sunglasses	**unas gafas de sol**
	*oo*nas g*a*f-as deh s*o*l
a sunshade	**una sombrilla**
	*oo*na sombr*ee*-ya
an umbrella	**un paraguas**
	oon pa-r*a*gwas
some writing paper	**papel de escribir**
	pap-*e*l deh escrib-*ee*r
I'd like . . . [*show the camera*]	Quiero . . .
	kee-*airo* . . .
a colour film	**un rollo en color**
	oon r*o*-yo en col-*o*r
a black and white film	**un rollo en blanco y negro**
	oon r*o*-yo en bl*a*nco ee n*e*g-ro
for prints	**para papel**
	p*a*ra pap-*e*l
for slides	**para diapositivas**
	p*a*ra dee-aposit*ee*bas
12 (24/36) exposures	**de doce (veinticuatro/treinta y seis) fotos**
	deh d*o*theh (beyntee-cw*a*tro/treynta-ee-s*e*ys) f*o*t-os
a standard 8mm film	**un rollo standard de ocho milimetros**
	oon r*o*-yo st*a*n-derd deh *o*ch-o mil*i*met-ros
a super 8 film	**un rollo super ocho**
	oon r*o*-yo s*oo*pair *o*ch-o

some flash bulbs	**unas bombillas de flash**
	_oo_nas bomb_ee_-yas deh fl_a_sh
This camera is broken	**Esta cámara esta rota**
	_e_sta c_a_mara est_a_ r_o_t-ah
The film is stuck	**El rollo esta atascado**
	el r_o_-yo est_a_ atasc_a_d-o
Please can you . . .	**Por favor, ¿puede . . .**
	por fab-_o_r pwed-eh . . .
develop/print this?	**revelar/imprimir esto?**
	rebel-_a_r/imprim-_ee_r _e_sto
load the camera for me?	**recargar mi cámara?**
	rek-arg_a_r mee c_a_mara

[For other essential expressions, see 'Shop talk', p. 54]

The tobacconist's

ESSENTIAL INFORMATION

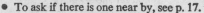

- Tobacco is sold where you see this sign which is red and yellow.
- A tobacconist's is called **ESTANCO** or **TABACALERA.**
- To ask if there is one near by, see p. 17.
- Tobacconist's always sell postage stamps, and you can even post your letters in some of them.
- They also sell lottery tickets and other items that you usually find in a stationer's.
- You can buy cigarettes as well in bars, supermarkets, at news-stands and kiosks.

WHAT TO SAY

A packet of cigarettes . . .	**Un paquete de cigarrillos . . .** oon pak*et*-eh deh thiggar*ee*-yos . . .
with filters	**con filtro** con f*i*ltro
without filters	**sin filtro** sin f*i*ltro
king size	**extra largos** *e*xtra l*a*rgos
menthol	**mentolados** mentola*d*-os
Those up there . . .	**Esos de allí . . .** *e*s-os deh a-y*ee* . . .
on the right	**a la derecha** ah la der*e*ch-ah
on the left	**a la izquierda** ah la ithk-y*air*da
These [*point*]	**Estos** *e*stos

Cigarettes, please ...
Cigarillos, por favor ...
thiggaree-yos por faƁ-or ...

100, 200, 300
cien, doscientos, trescientos
thee-en dos-thee-entos
tres-thee-entos

two packets
dos paquetes
dos paket-es

Have you got ...
¿Tiene ...
tee-en-eh ...

English cigarettes?
cigarillos ingleses?
thiggaree-yos in-gles-es

American cigarettes?
cigarrillos americanos?
thiggaree-yos americanos

English pipe tobacco?
tabaco de pipa inglés?
tabacco deh peepa in-gles

American pipe tobacco?
tabaco de pipa americano?
tabacco deh peepa americano

rolling tobacco?
picadura de tabaco?
picadoo-ra deh tabacco

A packet of pipe tobacco
Un paquete de tabaco de pipa
oon paket-eh deh tabacco deh
peepa

That one down there ...
Ese de allá abajo ...
es-eh deh a-ya aba-ho ...

on the right
a la derecha
ah la derech-ah

on the left
a la izquierda
ah la ithk-yairda

This one [*point*]
Este
esteh

A cigar, please
Un puro, por favor
oon poo-ro por fab-or

That one [*point*]
Ese
es-eh

Some cigars
Puros
poo-ros

Those [*point*]
Esos
es-os

A box of matches
Una caja de cerillas
oona ca-ha deh theree-yas

A packet of pipe-cleaners
[*Show lighter*]
Un paquete de escobillas
oon paket-eh deh escobee-yas

A packet of flints	**Un paquete de piedras de encendedor**
	oon pak*e*t-eh deh pee-*e*dras deh enthended*o*r
Lighter fuel	**Combustible para el encendedor**
	comboost*ee*bleh p*a*ra el enthended*o*r
Lighter gas, please	**Gas para el encendedor, por favor**
	g*a*s p*a*ra el enthended*o*r por fab-*o*r

[*For other essential expressions, see 'Shop talk', p. 54*]

Buying clothes

ESSENTIAL INFORMATION

● Look for:
  CONFECCIONES SEÑORA (women's clothes)
  SEDERIA (lingerie)
  BOUTIQUE
  MODAS (fashions)
  CONFECCIONES CABALLERO (men's clothes)
  SASTRERIA-PAÑERIA (men's clothes)
  ZAPATERIA/CALZADOS (shoe shop)
● If you are interested in leather and fur articles look for a **PELETERIA** or **CURTIDOS** or **ARTICULOS DE PIEL.**
● You can also buy clothes in the big stores: **ALMACENES** or **GALERIAS.**
● Don't buy without being measured first or without trying things on.
● Don't rely on conversion charts of clothing sizes (see p. 143).
● If you are buying for someone else, take their measurements with you.

WHAT TO SAY

I'd like ...	Quiero ...
	kee-*airo* ...
an anorak	un anorak
	oon anor*ak*
a belt	un cinturón
	oon thintoo-*ron*
a bikini	un bikini
	oon bik*ini*
a blouse	una blusa
	*oo*na bl*oo*sa
a bra	un sujetador
	oon soohet-ad*or*
a cap (swimming/skiing)	un gorro (de baño/de esquí)
	oon *gorro* (deh *ban*-yo/deh sk*i*)
a cardigan	una chaqueta de punto
	*oo*na chaket-ah deh p*oo*nto
a coat	un abrigo
	oon abr*eego*
a dress	un vestido
	oon best*eedo*
a hat	un sombrero
	oon sombr*airo*
a jacket	una chaqueta
	*oo*na chaket-ah
a jumper	un jersey
	oon hair-s*ay*
a nightdress	un camisón
	oon camis*on*
a pair of pyjamas	un pijama
	oon peeh*am*-ah
a pullover	un jersey
	oon hair-s*ay*
a raincoat	un impermeable
	oon impairmch-*ab*-leh
a shirt	una camisa
	*oo*na cam*eesa*
a skirt	una falda
	*oo*na f*alda*
a suit	un traje
	oon tr*a*-heh

I'd like ...   **Quiero ...**
                                    kee-*airo* ...
  a swimsuit   **un traje de baño**
                                    oon tra-heh deh ban-yo
  a T-shirt   **una camiseta**
                                    *oo*na cami-set-ah
I'd like a pair of ...   **Quiero un par de ...**
                                    kee-*airo* oon par deh ...
  briefs (women)   **bragas**
                                    br*a*gas
  gloves   **guantes**
                                    gwan-tes
  jeans   **vaqueros**
                                    bak-*airo*s
  shorts   **pantalones cortos**
                                    pantalon-es cortos
  socks (short/long)   **calcetines (cortos/largos)**
                                    caltheteen-es (cortos/largos)
  stockings   **medias**
                                    med-yas
  tights   **leotardos**
                                    leotardos
  trousers   **pantalones**
                                    pantalon-es
  underpants (men)   **calzoncillos**
                                    calthonth*ee*-yos
I'd like a pair of ...   **Quiero un par de ...**
                                    kee-*airo* oon par deh ...
  shoes   **zapatos**
                                    thap*a*t-os
  canvas shoes   **zapatos de lona**
                                    thap*a*t-os deh lon-ah
  sandals   **sandalias**
                                    sand*a*l-yas
  beach shoes   **playeras**
                                    pla-y*airr*as
  smart shoes   **zapatos de vestir**
                                    thap*a*t-os deh best*ee*r
  boots   **botas**
                                    bot-as
  moccasins   **mocasines**
                                    moccasin-es

My size is . . . (clothes)	**Mi talla es . . .**
	mee ta-ya es
My size is . . . (shoes)	**Mi número es . . .**
	mee noomairo es . . .
Can you measure me, please?	**¿Puede medirme, por favor?**
	pwed-eh medeermeh por fab-or
Can I try it on?	**¿Puedo probármelo?**
	pwed-o probarmeh-lo
It's for a present	**Es para un regalo**
	es para oon reg-al-o
These are the measurements . . .	**Estas son las medidas . . .**
[Show written]	estas son las medeedas . . .
bust	**busto**
	boosto
chest	**pecho**
	pech-o
collar	**cuello**
	cwel-yo
hip	**cadera**
	cadaira
leg	**pierna**
	pee-airna
waist	**cintura**
	thin-toora
Have you got something . . .	**¿Tiene algo . . .**
	tee-en-eh algo . . .
in black ?	**en negro?**
	en neg-ro
in white?	**en blanco?**
	en blanco
in grey?	**en gris?**
	en grees
in blue?	**en azul?**
	en athool
in brown?	**en marrón?**
	en marron
in pink?	**en rosa?**
	en ros-ah
in green?	**en verde?**
	en bair-deh
in red?	**en rojo?**
	en ro-ho

Have you got something . . .	¿Tiene algo . . .
	tee-*en*-eh *a*lgo . . .
in yellow?	**en amarillo?**
	en amar*ee*-yo
in this colour? [*point*]	**en este color?**
	en *e*steh co*lor*
in cotton?	**en algodón?**
	en algod*on*
in denim?	**en dril?**
	en dr*i*l
in leather?	**en cuero?**
	en cw*air*o
in nylon?	**en nylon?**
	en n*y*lon
in suede?	**en ante?**
	en *a*nteh
in wool?	**en lana?**
	en l*a*n-ah
in this material? [*point*]	**en este material?**
	en *e*steh ma-teri-*a*l

[*For other essential expressions, see 'Shop talk', p. 54*]

Replacing equipment

ESSENTIAL INFORMATION

- Look for these shops and signs:
  FERRETERIA (hardware)
  ELECTRODOMESTICOS (electrical goods)
  DROGUERIA (household cleaning materials)
- In a supermarket or department store look for these signs:
  HOGAR, or **ARTICULOS PARA EL HOGAR** and
  ARTICULOS DE LIMPIEZA.
- To ask the way to the shop, see p. 17.
- At a campsite try their shop first.

WHAT TO SAY

Have you got ...   ¿Tiene ...
                                 tec-*en*-eh ...

an adaptor   **un adaptador?**
[*show appliance*]   oon adapta-d*o*r

a bottle of butane gas?   **una botella de gas butano?**
                                 *oo*na botel-ya deh gas bootan-o

a bottle of propane gas?   **una botella de gas propano?**
                                 *oo*na botel-ya deh gas propan-o

a bottle opener?   **un abrebotellas?**
                                 oon abreh-botel-yas

a corkscrew?   **un sacacorchos?**
                                 oon sac-acorchos

any disinfectant?   **desinfectante?**
                                 des-infectanteh

any disposable cups?   **vasos de papel?**
                                 bas-os deh pap-*el*

any disposable plates?   **platos de papel?**
                                 pl*a*t-os deh pap-*el*

a drying up cloth?   **un paño de cocina?**
                                 oon p*a*n-yo deh coth*ee*na

any forks?   **tenedores?**
                                 ten-ed-*o*r-es

a fuse? [*show old one*]   **un fusible?**
                                 oon foos*ee*bleh

an insecticide spray?   **un insecticida en spray?**
                                 oon insecti-th*ee*da en spr*a*-ee

a paper kitchen roll?   **un rollo de papel de cocina?**
                                 oon r*o*-yo deh pap-*el* deh coth*ee*na

any knives?   **cuchillos?**
                                 cooch*ee*-yos

a light bulb? [*show old   **una bombilla?**
one*]   *oo*na bombee-ya

a plastic bucket?   **un cubo de plástico?**
                                 oon c*oo*bo deh pl*a*stico

a plastic can?   **una lata de plástico?**
                                 *oo*na l*a*t-ah deh pl*a*stico

a scouring pad?   **un estropajo?**
                                 oon estrop*a*-ho

a spanner?   **una llave inglesa?**
                                 *oo*na y*a*b-eh in-gles-ah

Have you got ...	**¿Tiene ...**
	tee-*en*-eh ...
a sponge?	**una esponja?**
	*oo*na espong-ha
any string?	**cuerda?**
	cw*air*da
any tent pegs?	**estacas de camping?**
	est*ac*-as deh c*a*mping
a tin opener?	**un abrelatas?**
	oon abrel-*at*-as
a torch?	**una linterna?**
	*oo*na lint*air*na
any torch batteries?	**pilas de linterna?**
[*show old ones*]	p*ee*las deh lint*air*na
a universal plug (for the sink)?	**un tapón universal (para la fregadera)?**
	oon tap-*on* oonibair-s*a*l p*a*ra la freg-ad*ai*ra
a washing line?	**un tendedero?**
	oon tended-*air*o
any washing powder?	**detergente?**
	det-air-h*e*nteh
any washing-up liquid?	**lavavajillas?**
	lababa-h*ee*-yas
a washing-up brush?	**un cepillo para fregar los platos?**
[*For other essential expressions, see 'Shop talk', p. 54*]	oon thep*ee*-yo p*a*ra freg*a*r los pl*a*t-os

Shop talk

ESSENTIAL INFORMATION

- Know your coins and notes
  coins: see illustration
  notes: 100 pesetas, 500, 1000 and 5000 pesetas

● Know how to say the important weights and measures

50 grams	**cincuenta gramos**
	thin-cwenta gram-os
100 grams	**cien gramos**
	thee-*en* gram-os
200 grams	**doscientos gramos**
	dos-thee-*e*ntos gram-os
½ kilo	**medio kilo**
	med-yo k*i*lo
1 kilo	**un kilo**
	oon k*i*lo
2 kilos	**dos kilos**
	dos k*i*los
½ litre	**medio litro**
	med-yo l*i*tro
1 litre	**un litro**
	oon l*i*tro
2 litres	**dos litros**
[*For numbers, see p. 131*]	dos l*i*tros

● In small shops don't be surprised if the customers, as well as the shop assistant, say 'hello' and 'good-bye' to you.

Customer

Hello	**Hola**
	o-la
Good morning	**Buenos días**
	bwen-os dee*a*s
Good afternoon	**Buenas tardes**
	bwen-as t*a*rd-es
Good-bye	**Adiós**
	ad-y*o*s
I'm just looking	**Sólo estoy mirando**
	sol-o estoy mirr*a*ndo
Excuse me	**Perdone**
	paird*o*n-eh
How much is this/that?	**¿Cuánto es esto/eso?**
	cw*a*nto es esto/es-o
What is that?	**¿Qué es eso?**
	keh es es-o
What are those?	**¿Qué son esos?**
	keh son es-os
Is there a discount?	**¿Hay descuento?**
	*a*h-ee des-cwento

I'd like that, please	**Quiero eso, por favor**
	kee-*air*o es-o por fab-*or*
Not that	**Eso no**
	es-o no
Like that	**Así**
	a*see*
That's enough, thank you	**Basta, gracias**
	basta grath-yas
More, please	**Mas, por favor**
	mas por fab-*or*
Less, please	**Menos, por favor**
	men-os por fab-*or*
That's fine	**Eso está bien**
	es-o esta bee-*en*
OK	**Está bien**
	esta bee-*en*
I won't take it, thank you	**No lo tomo, gracias**
	no lo tom-o grath-yas
It's not right	**No está bien**
	no esta bee-*en*
Thank you very much	**Muchas gracias**
	*moo*chas grath-yas
Have you got something ...	**¿Tiene algo ...**
	tee-en-eh *a*lgo ...
better?	**mejor?**
	m*eh*-hor
cheaper?	**mas barato?**
	mas ba-*rat*-o
different?	**diferente?**
	diffair-enteh
larger?	**mas grande?**
	mas grandeh
smaller?	**mas pequeño?**
	mas peken-yo
At what time do you ...	**¿A qué hora ...**
	ah k*eh* *o*ra ...
open?	**abren?**
	*a*b-ren
close?	**cierran?**
	thee-erran
Can I have a bag, please?	**¿Puedo tener una bolsa, por favor?**
	pwed-o ten-*air* *oo*na bolsa por fab-*or*

Can you give me a receipt?	**¿Puede darme un recibo?**
	pwed-eh darmeh oon retheebo
Do you take ...	**¿Toman ustedes ...**
	tom-an oosted-es ...
English/American money?	**dinero inglés/americano?**
	din-airo in-gles/americano
travellers' cheques?	**cheques de viaje?**
	chek-es deh bee-ah-heh
credit cards?	**tarjetas de crédito?**
	tarhet-as deh credit-o
I'd like ...	**Quiero ...**
	kee-airo ...
one like that	**uno así**
	oono asee
two like that	**dos así**
	dos asee

Shop assistant

Can I help you?	**¿En qué puedo servirle?**
	en keh pwed-o sairbeer-leh
What would you like?	**¿Qué desea/quiere?**
	keh des-eh-ah/kee-aireh
Will that be all?	**¿Será eso todo?**
	serra es-o tod-o
Is that all?	**¿Eso es todo?**
	es-o es tod-o
Anything else?	**¿Algo mas?**
	algo mas
Would you like it wrapped?	**¿Quiere que se lo envuelva?**
	kee-aireh keh seh lo enbwelba
Sorry, none left	**Lo siento, no queda ninguno**
	lo see-ento no ked-ah nin-goono
I haven't got any	**No tengo**
	no tengo
I haven't got any more	**No tengo mas**
	no tengo mas
How many do you want?	**¿Cuántos quiere?**
	cwantos kee-aireh
How much do you want?	**¿Cuánto quiere?**
	cwanto kee-aireh
Is that enough?	**¿Basta?**
	basta

Shopping for food

Bread

ESSENTIAL INFORMATION

- Finding a baker's, see p. 17.
- Key words to look for:
  HORNO (baker's)
  PANADERIA (baker's)
  PANADERO (baker)
  PAN (bread)
- Supermarkets of any size and general stores nearly always sell bread.
- Panaderías, as well as other shops, are open from 9 a.m. – 1 p.m. and from 4 p.m. – 8 p.m. closing at lunchtime. In popular resorts, the shops often remain open all day.
- The most characteristic type of loaf is the **barra** which is a wider version of the 'french stick', and comes in different sizes according to the weight.
- For any other type of loaf, say **un pan** (oon pan), and point.
- In some bakers' you can buy milk; look for this sign: **LECHERIA-PANADERIA**. Soft drinks, sweets and ice-creams can also be bought here.
- It's quite usual in Spain to have your bread delivered; if you wish to take advantage of this service, simply have a word with your local baker. You only have to say: **¿Puede traer el pan a casa?** (pwed-eh tra-*air* el pana cas-a).

WHAT TO SAY

Some bread, please	**Pan, por favor**
	pan for fab-*or*
A loaf (like that)	**Un pan (así)**
	oon pan (as*ee*)
One long loaf	**Una barra**
	*oo*na barra
Three loaves	**Tres panes**
	tres pan-es

Four long loaves	**Cuatro barras**
	cwatro barras
250 grams of ...	**Doscientos cincuenta gramos de ...**
	dos-thee-entos thin-cwenta ...
	gram-os deh ...
½ kilo of ...	**Medio kilo de ...**
	med-yo kilo deh ...
1 kilo of ...	**Un kilo de ...**
	oon kilo deh ...
A bread roll	**Un panecillo**
	oon pannethee-yo
Four bread rolls	**Cuatro panecillos**
	cwatro pannethee-yos
Four crescent rolls	**Cuatro croissants**
	cwatro crwassans
A packet of ...	**Un paquete de ...**
	oon paket-eh deh ...
English bread	**pan de molde**
	pan deh moldeh
toasted bread	**pan tostado**
	pan tostad-o
brown bread	**pan integral**
	pan inteh-gral

[*For other essential expressions, see 'Shop talk', p. 54*]

Cakes

ESSENTIAL INFORMATION

- Key words to look for:
  PASTELERIA (cake shop)
  CONFITERIA (confectionery, they also sell cakes)
  PASTELERO (cake/pastry maker)
  PASTELES (cakes)
  PASTAS (pastries)
- **CHURRERIA**: a place to buy **churros**, a kind of fritter that can be eaten on its own (takeaway) or dipped in hot thick chocolate. You have to ask for: **chocolate con churros.**
- **CAFETERIA**: a place where you can buy cakes, as well as drinks. You can also have chocolate and **churros.** See p. 80 'Ordering a drink'.
- To find a cake shop, see p. 17

WHAT TO SAY

The type of cakes you find in the shops varies from region to region but the following are some of the most common.

un churro oon ch*oo*ro	a finger-size fritter
un buñuelo oon boon-yoo-*el*-o	a round fritter
magdalenas magda-*len*-as	madeleines (small sponge teacakes)
una ensaimada oona en-sa-ee-m*ad*-ah	a bun made of puff pastry covered with sugar icing and filled with cream
mantecado el manteh-c*ad*-o	shortbread
turrón too-ron	nougat (can be hard or soft)
el mazapán el matha-p*an*	marzipan
una yema oona y*em*-ah	a candied egg yolk

una rosquilla   **a ring-shaped roll (like a**
oona ros-*kee*-ya   **doughnut)**
un merengue   **a meringue**
oon meh-ren-geh

You usually buy medium-size cakes by number:

one doughnut	**un donut**
	oon d*o*n-oot
two doughnuts, please	**dos donuts, por favor**
	dos d*o*n-oots por fab-*or*

You buy small cakes by weight:

200 grams of cream puffs	**doscientos gramos de pastelitos de crema**
	dos-thee-*en*tos gr*a*m-os deh pastel-*ee*tos deh crem-ah
400 grams of biscuits	**cuatrocientos gramos de galletas**
	cwatro-thee-*en*tos gr*a*m-os deh ga-*yet*-as

You may want to buy a larger cake by the slice:

one slice of apple cake	**un trozo de pastel de manzana**
	oon tr*o*th-o deh pastel deh manth*a*na
two slices of almond cake	**dos trozos de pastel de almendra**
	dos tr*o*th-os deh pastel deh alm*e*ndra

You buy **churros** by pesetas:

20 pesetas of churros, please	**veinte pesetas de churros, por favor**
	b*e*yn-teh pes-*et*-as deh ch*oo*-ros por fab-*or*

You may also want to say:

a selection, please	**pasteles variados, por favor**
	pastel-es baree-*ad*-os por fab-*or*

[*For other essential expressions, see 'Shop talk', p. 54*]

Ice-cream and sweets

ESSENTIAL INFORMATION

- Key words to look for:
  HELADOS (ice-creams)
  HELADERO (ice-cream maker/seller)
  HELADERIA (ice-cream shop/parlour)
  HORCHATERIA (ice-cream shop which also sells soft ice drinks)
  CONFITERIA (sweet and cake shop)
  BOMBONERIA (sweet shop)
  CONFITERO (sweet maker/seller)
  PASTELERIA (cake shop)
  PASTELERO (cake/pastry maker)
- Best known ice-cream brand names:
  FRIGO   **LAR**
  CAMI   **LIC**
  LIDO   **ITALIANOS**
- Prepacked sweets are available in general stores and supermarkets and usually in **PANADERIAS** (bakers'), where you can also buy ice-creams.
- You can also buy sweets in kiosks and in the tobacconist's.

WHAT TO SAY

A . . . ice, please	**Un helado de . . . , por favor**
	oon elad-o deh . . . por fab-or
chocolate	**chocolate**
	chocolat-eh
pistachio	**mantecado**
	manteh-cad-o
raspberry	**frambuesa**
	frambwessa
strawberry	**fresa**
	fressa
vanilla	**vainilla**
	banee-ya
coffee	**café**
	cafeh

A ... ice, please	**Un helado de ...**, por favor
	oon el*a*d-o deh ... por fab-*or*
nougat flavour	**turrón**
	too-r*on*
lemon	**limón**
	lim-*on*
orange	**naranja**
	na-r*a*ng-ha
tuttifrutti	**tuttifrutti**
	toottifr*oo*tti
creamy	**nata**
	n*a*-ta
hazelnut	**avellana**
	ab-*el*-yanna
mint	**menta**
	m*e*nta
croccanti	**croccanti**
	crocc*a*nti
A single	**Uno sencillo**
[*specify flavour as above*]	*oo*no senth*ee*-yo
Two singles	**Dos sencillos**
	dos senth*ee*-yos
A double	**Uno doble**
	*oo*no d*o*bleh
Two doubles	**Dos dobles**
	dos d*o*bles
A cone	**Un barquillo**
	oon bark*ee*-yo
An iced lolly	**Un polo**
	oon p*o*l-o
A chocolate iced lolly	**Un polo de bombón**
	oon p*o*l-o de bomb*on*
A wafer	**Un corte**
	oon c*o*rteh
A lollipop	**Un pirulí**
	oon piroo*lee*
A tub	**Un Cami**
	oon c*a*-mee
A cake with ice-cream	**Una tarta helada**
	*oo*na t*a*rta el*a*dda
A packet of ...	**Un paquete de ...**
	oon pak*et*-eh deh ...
chewing gum	**chicle**
	ch*ee*-cleh

100 grams of ...	**Cien gramos de ...**
	thee-*en* gram-os deh ...
200 grams of ...	**Doscientos gramos de ...**
	dos-thee-*en*tos gram-os deh ...
sweets	**caramelos**
	caram*el*-os
toffees	**pastillas de café con leche**
	past*ee*-yas deh caf*eh* con *lech*-eh
chocolates	**bombones**
	bomb*on*-es
mints	**caramelos de menta**
[*For other essential*	caram*el*-os deh menta
expressions, see 'Shop talk', p. 54]	

In the supermarket

ESSENTIAL INFORMATION

- The place to ask for: [*see p. 17*]

  UN SUPERMERCADO (supermarket)
  UN AUTOSERVICIO (corner self-service)
  ALIMENTACION GENERAL (general food store)
- You may see outside the shop the words: **SPAR** or **VEGE.**
- Key instructions on signs in the shop:
  ENTRADA (entrance)
  PROHIBIDA LA ENTRADA (no entry)
  SALIDA (exit)
  PROHIBIDA LA SALIDA (no exit)
  SIN SALIDA (no way out)
  SALIDA SIN COMPRAS (exit for non-buyers)
  CAJA (check-out, cash desk)
  EN OFERTA (on offer)
  AUTOSERVICIO (self-service)
- Supermarkets are open from 9 a.m. – 1 p.m. and from 4 p.m. – 8 p.m., but in some places, especially in holiday resorts and in the summer, supermarkets, as well as other shops, stay open at lunchtime.
- No need to say anything in a supermarket, but ask if you can't see what you want.

WHAT TO SAY

Excuse me, please	**Perdone, por favor**
	pairdon-eh por fab-or
Where is ...	**¿Dónde está ...**
	dondeh esta ...
the bread?	**el pan?**
	el pan
the butter?	**la mantequilla?**
	la manteh-kee-ya
the cheese?	**el queso?**
	el kes-o
the chocolate?	**el chocolate?**
	el chocolat-eh
the coffee?	**el café?**
	el cafeh
the cooking oil?	**el aceite?**
	el athay-teh
the fish (fresh)?	**el pescado?**
	el pescad-o
the fruit?	**la fruta?**
	la froota
the jam?	**la mermelada?**
	la mairmel-ad-ah
the meat?	**la carne?**
	la carneh
the milk?	**la leche?**
	la lech-eh
the mineral water?	**el agua mineral?**
	el agwa mineral
the salt?	**la sal?**
	la sal
the sugar?	**el azúcar?**
	el athoocar
the tea?	**el té?**
	el teh
the tinned fish?	**el pescado en lata?**
	el pescad-o en lat-ah
the tinned fruit?	**la fruta en lata?**
	la froota en lat-ah
the vinegar?	**el vinagre?**
	el beenag-reh

the wine?	**el vino?**
	el beeno
the yogurt?	**el yogurt?**
	el yogoort
Where are ...	**¿Dónde están ...**
	dondeh estan ...
the biscuits?	**las galletas?**
	las ga-yettas
the crisps?	**las patatas fritas?**
	las patat-as freetas
the eggs?	**los huevos?**
	los web-os
the frozen foods?	**los congelados?**
	los conhellad-os
the fruit juices?	**los zumos de fruta?**
	los thoom-os dch froota
the pastas?	**las pastas?**
	las pastas
the seafoods?	**los mariscos?**
	los ma-riskos
the snails?	**los caracoles?**
	los caracol-es
the soft drinks?	**las bebidas sin alcohol?**
	las bebeedas sin alco-ol
the sweets?	**los caramelos?**
	los caramel-os
the tinned vegetables?	**las verduras en lata?**
	las bairdoo-ras en lat-ah
the vegetables?	**las verduras?**
	las bairdoo-ras

[For other essential expressions, see 'Shop talk', p. 54]

Picnic food

ESSENTIAL INFORMATION

- Key words to look for:
  CHARCUTERIA (pork butcher's delicatessen)
  EMBUTIDOS (cold meat sausages)
  FIAMBRES (cold meat, cold cuts)
  TIENDA DE ULTRAMARINOS (grocer's)
  MANTEQUERIA (delicatessen)
  CARNECERIA (butcher's)
- In these shops you can buy a wide variety of food such as ham, salami, cheese, olives, appetizers, sausages and freshly made takeaway dishes. Specialities differ from region to region.
- Weight guide:
  4–6oz/150g of prepared salad per two people, if eaten as a starter to a substantial meal.
  3–4oz/100g of prepared salad per person, if eaten as the main part of a picnic-type meal.

WHAT TO SAY

A slice of ...	Una rodaja de ...
	*oo*na rod-*a*ha deh ...
Two slices of ...	Dos rodajas de ...
	dos rod-*a*has deh ...
salami	salchichón
	salcheech*o*n
spicy hard sausage	chorizo
	chor-*ee*tho
pâté	paté
	pat*e*h
ham	jamón de york
	ham-*o*n deh york
cured ham, thinly sliced	jamón serrano
	ham-*o*n serr*a*nno
pork and beef cold meat	mortadela
	morta-d*e*lla

stuffed turkey	**pavo trufado**
	pab-o troofad-o
100 grams of ...	**Cien gramos de ...**
	thee-en gram-os deh ...
150 grams of ...	**Ciento cincuenta gramos de ...**
	thee-ento thin-cwenta gram-os deh ...
200 grams of ...	**Doscientos gramos de ...**
	dos-thee-entos gram-os deh ...
300 grams of ...	**Trescientos gramos de ...**
	tres-thee-entos gram-os deh ...
Russian salad	**ensalada rusa**
	ensalad-ah roosa
tomato salad	**ensalada de tomate**
	ensalad-ah deh tomat-eh
olives	**olivas**
	oleebas
anchovies	**anchoas**
	ancho-as
cheese	**queso**
	kes-o

You may also like to try some of these:

pizza	pizza
pizza	
salchicha de frankfurt	frankfurter
salcheecha deh frankfort	
pollo asado	roast chicken
pol-yo asad-o	
morcilla	black pudding
morthee-ya	
palitos de queso	cheese sticks
paleetos deh kes-o	
cortezas	pork crackling/scratchings
corteth-as	
puntas de espárragos	asparagus tips
poontas deh espuragos	
salmón ahumado	smoked salmon
sal-mon ah-oomad-o	
butifarra	spiced sausage
booti-farra	
longaniza	highly-seasoned sausage made
longa-neetha	with pork and herbs

olivas rellenas	stuffed olives
ol*ee*bas reh-*yen*-as	
olivas negras	black olives
ol*ee*bas *neg*-ras	
patatas fritas	crisps
pat*at*-as fr*ee*tas	
pepinillos	gherkins
peppin*ee*-yos	
galletas saladas	crackers
ga-*yet*-as sal*ad*-as	
sardinas en aceite	sardines in oil
sard*ee*nas en ath*ay*-teh	
sardinas rancias	dry salty sardines
sard*ee*nas r*a*nth-yas	
atún	tuna
at*oo*n	
queso de Burgos	soft, creamy cheese
kes-o deh b*oo*rgos	
queso manchego	hard cheese from ewe's milk
kes-o manch*eg*-o	
queso de roncal	salted, smoked cheese made from
kes-o deh ronc*al*	ewe's milk
queso de bola	a round-shaped, mild cheese
kes-o deh b*ol*-ah	
queso de cabra	goat cheese
kes-o deh c*a*bra	
queso de teta	a firm, bland cheese made from
kes-o deh t*e*ta	cow's milk

[*For other essential expressions, see 'Shop talk', p. 54*]

Fruit and vegetables

ESSENTIAL INFORMATION

- Key words to look for: **VERDURA** (vegetables)
  FRUTA (fruit) **LEGUMBRES** (vegetables)
  FRUTERO (fruit seller) **VERDULERIA** (vegetable shop)
  FRUTERIA (fruit shop) **FRESCO** (an indication of freshness)
- If possible, buy fruit and vegetables in the market where they are cheaper and fresher than in the shops. Open-air markets are held once or twice a week in most areas (or daily in large towns), usually in the mornings.
- It is customary for you to choose your own fruit and vegetables in the market (and in some shops) and for the stallholder to weigh and price them. You must take your own shopping bag: paper and plastic bags are not normally provided.
- Weight guide: 1 kilo of potatoes is sufficient for six people for one meal.

WHAT TO SAY

½ kilo (1lb) of ...	**Medio kilo de ...**
	med-yo *k*ilo deh ...
1 kilo of ...	**Un kilo de ...**
	oon *k*ilo deh ...
2 kilos of ...	**Dos kilos de ...**
	dos *k*ilos deh ...
apples	**manzanas**
	manth*a*nas
bananas	**plátanos**
	pl*a*ttan-os
cherries	**cerezas**
	ther*e*th-as
figs	**higos**
	ee-gos
grapes (black/white)	**uvas (blancas/negras)**
	*oo*bas (blancas/n*e*g-ras)
oranges	**naranjas**
	na-r*a*ng-has
pears	**peras**
	p*e*rras

2 kilos of ...	**Dos kilos de ...**
	dos kilos deh ...
peaches	**melocotones**
	mellocoton-es
plums	**ciruelas**
	theer-rwellas
strawberries	**fresas**
	fressas
A pineapple, please	**Una piña, por favor**
	oona peen-ya por fab-or
A grapefruit	**Un pomelo**
	oon pomello
A melon	**Un melón**
	oon melon
A water-melon	**Una sandía**
	oona sandeea
250 grams of ...	**Doscientos cincuenta gramos de ...**
	dos-thee-entos thin-cwenta gram-os deh ...
½ kilo of ...	**Medio kilo de ...**
	med-yo kilo deh ...
1 kilo of ...	**Un kilo de ...**
	oon kilo deh ...
1½ kilos of ...	**Un kilo y medio de ...**
	oon kilo ee med-yo deh ...
2 kilos of ...	**Dos kilos de ...**
	dos kilos deh ...
artichokes	**alcachofas**
	alkachoffas
asparagus	**esparrago**
	esparrago
broad beans	**habas**
	abbas
carrots	**zanahorias**
	thanna-oree-as
green beans	**judías verdes**
	hoodee-as bair-des
leeks	**puerros**
	pwerros
mushrooms	**champiñones**
	champin-yon-es

onions	**cebollas**
	the*bol*-yas
peas	**guisantes**
	ghiss*ant*-es
potatoes	**patatas**
	pat*at*-as
shallots	**chalotes**
	chall*ot*-es
spinach	**espinacas**
	espin*ac*-as
tomatoes	**tomates**
	tom*at*-es
A bunch of ...	**Un puñado de ...**
	oon poon-y*ad*-o deh ...
parsley	**perejil**
	perreh*il*
radishes	**rábanos**
	rab-annos
A head of garlic	**Una cabeza de ajo**
	*oo*na cabeth-ah deh *ah*-ho
A lettuce	**Una lechuga**
	oona lech*oo*ga
A cauliflower	**Una coliflor**
	*oo*na colliflor
A cabbage	**Un repollo**
	oon rep*ol*-yo
A cucumber	**Un pepino**
	oon pep*ee*no
Like that, please	**Así, por favor**
	a*see* por fab-*or*

Some fruit and vegetables with which you may not be familiar:

acelgas	chard, a kind of beet with edible
athelgas	stalks and leaves
calabaza	pumpkin, orange coloured fruit
calab*atha*	with edible layer next to rind
caqui	date plum: soft sweet winter
c*a*-kee	fruit like a large tomato
escarola	endive, a salad plant, also called
escar*ol*-ah	'chicory'
granada	pomegranate, a fruit, orange in
gran*ad*-ah	colour, with lots of seeds

higo chumbo	prickly pear, as its name suggests,
ee-go ch*oo*mbo	the fruit of a cactus
membrillo	quince, a pear shaped fruit used as
membr*ee*-yo	a preserve
níspero	medlar/loquat, small, slightly
n*ee*espero	sour fruit, orange in colour and
	juicy

[*For other essential expressions, see 'Shop talk', p. 54*]

Meat

ESSENTIAL INFORMATION

- Key words to look for:
  CARNECERIA (butcher's)
  CARNICERO (butcher)
- Weight guide: 4–6oz/125–200g of meat per person for one meal.
- The diagrams opposite are to help you make sense of labels on counters and supermarket displays, and decide which cut or joint to have. Translations do not help, and you don't need to say the Spanish word involved.

WHAT TO SAY

For a joint, choose the type of meat and then say how many people it is for:

Some beef, please	**Buey, por favor**
	bw*ay* por fab*o*r
Some lamb/young lamb	**Cordero/ternasco**
	cord*airo*/tairn*a*sco
Some mutton	**Carnero/oveja**
	carn*airo*/obeh-ha

Beef Buey

1 Cuello
2 Espaldilla
3 Pecho
4 Morcillo
5 Lomo alto
6 Solomillo
7 Lomo bajo
8 Tapa
9 Cadera
10 Redondo
11 Contra
12 Babilla
13 Falda con costillar
14 Culeta

Veal Ternera

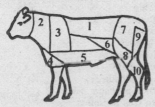

1 Lomo
2 Cuello
3 Espaldilla
4 Aleta o pecho
5 Falda
6 Riñonada
7 Cadera
8 Babilla
9 Contra
10 Morcillo (osso bucco)

Pork Cerdo

1 Aguja
2 Paletilla
3 Tocino
4 Chuletas o cinta
5 Magro para salchichas
6 Panceta
7 Jamón
8 Manos

Mutton Carnero/Oveja

1 Lomo
2 Costillar
3 Falda
4 Pecina
5 Paletilla
6 Cuello
7 Manos

Some pork

Cerdo
th*airdo*

Some veal

Ternera
tairn*aira*

A joint ...

Un asado ...
oon as*ado* ...

for two people

para dos personas
p*ara* dos pairs*on*-as

for four people

para cuatro personas
p*ara* c*watro* pairson-as

for six people

para seis personas
p*ara* s*eys* pairson-as

For steak, liver or kidneys, do as above:

Some steak, please

Bistec, por favor
bist*ec* por fab-*or*

Some liver

Hígado
*ee*ga-do

Some kidneys

Riñones
rin-*yon*-es

Some sausages

Salchichas
salch*ee*chas

Some mince ...

Carne picada ...
c*arne*h peec*ada* ...

for three people

para tres personas
p*ara* tres pairson-as

for five people

para cinco personas
p*ara* th*inko* pairson-as

For chops do it this way:

Two veal escalopes

Dos escalopes de ternera
dos escal*op*-es deh tairn*aira*

Three pork chops

Tres chuletas de cerdo
tres chool*etta*s deh th*airdo*

Four mutton chops

Cuatro chuletas de oveja
c*watro* chool*etta*s deh ob*eh*-ha

Five lamb chops

Cinco chuletas de cordero
th*inko* chool*etta*s deh cord*airo*

You may also want:

A chicken

Un pollo
oon p*ol*-yo

A rabbit	**Un conejo**
	oon conneh-ho
A tongue	**Una lengua**
	oona len-gwa

Other essential expressions [*see also p. 54*]

Please can you ...	**Por favor, ¿puede usted ...**
	por fab-or pwed-eh oosted ...
mince it?	**picarlo?**
	peecarlo
dice it?	**cortarlo en trozos?**
	cortarlo en troth-os
trim the fat?	**quitar la grasa?**
	keetar la grassa

Fish

ESSENTIAL INFORMATION

- The place to ask for:
  UNA PESCADERIA (fish shop)
- Markets and large supermarkets usually have a fresh fish stall.
- Another key word to look for is **MARISCOS** (seafood)
- Weight guide: 8oz/250g minimum per person, for one meal, of fish bought on the bone.
  i.e. ½ kilo/500g   for 2 people
      1 kilo   for 4 people
      1½ kilos   for 6 people

WHAT TO SAY

Purchase large fish and small shellfish by weight:

½ kilo of ...	**Medio kilo de ...**
	med-yo kilo deh ...
1 kilo of ...	**Un kilo de ...**
	oon kilo deh ...

1½ kilos of . . .	**Un kilo y medio de . . .**
	oon k*i*lo ee m*e*d-yo deh . . .
clams	**almejas**
	almeh-has
cod	**bacalao**
	bakkal*a*-o
hake	**merluza**
	mairl*oo*tha
mussels	**mejillones**
	mehee-y*o*n-es
prawns	**gambas**
	g*a*mbas
sardines	**sardinas**
	sard*ee*nas
shrimps (two names)	**camarones/quisquillas**
	cammar*o*n-es/kisk*ee*-yas
sprats	**sardinetas**
	sardin*e*ttas
turbot	**rodaballo**
	roddab*a*-yo
whitebait	**boquerones**
	bokeh-r*o*n-es

Some large fish can be purchased by the slice:

One slice of . . .	**Una rodaja de . . .**
	*oo*na rodd*a*-ha deh . . .
Two slices of . . .	**Dos rodajas de . . .**
	dos rodd*a*-has deh . . .
Six slices of . . .	**Seis rodajas de . . .**
	s*e*ys rodd*a*-has deh . . .
salmon	**salmón**
	sal-mon
cod	**bacalao**
	bakkal*a*-o
fresh tuna	**bonito**
	bon*ee*to
sea bream	**besugo**
	bes*oo*go

For some shellfish and 'frying pan' fish, specify the number:

A crab, please	**Un cangrejo, por favor**
	oon cangreh-ho por fab-*or*
A lobster	**Una langosta**
	*oo*na lan-g*o*sta
A plaice	**Un gallo**
	oon g*a*l-yo
A whiting	**Una pescadilla**
	*oo*na pescad*ee*-ya
A trout	**Una trucha**
	*oo*na tr*oo*cha
A sole	**Un lenguado**
	oon len-gw*a*ddo
A mackerel	**Una caballa**
	*oo*na cab*a*l-ya
A herring	**Un arenque**
	oon arr*e*nkeh
An octopus	**Un pulpo**
	oon p*oo*lpo
A carp	**Una carpa**
	*oo*na c*a*rpa

Other essential expressions [*see also p. 54*]

Please can you . . .	**Por favor, ¿puede . . .**
	por fab-*or* pwed-eh . . .
take the heads off?	**quitar las cabezas?**
	keet*ar* las cab-*eth*-as
clean them?	**limpiarlos?**
	limp-y*ar*-los
fillet them?	**quitar la espina?**
	keet*ar* la esp*ee*na

Eating and drinking out

Ordering a drink

ESSENTIAL INFORMATION

- The places to ask for: [*see p. 17*]
  UNA CAFETERIA (a more luxurious and modern café)
  UN CAFÉ
  UN BAR
- If you want to try Spanish wine and **tapas** in a typically Spanish atmosphere the places to go are: **UNA TASCA, UNA BODEGA, UN MESON** or **UNA TABERNA.** Usually you'll find all these places in the same area and it is the custom to make a tour of several local bars having one or two drinks in each.
- By law, the price list of drinks (**TARIFA** or **LISTA DE PRECIOS**) must be displayed outside or in the window.
- There is waiter service in all cafés, but you can drink at the bar or counter if you wish (cheaper).
- Always leave a tip of 10% to 15% of the bill unless you see **SERVICIO INCLUIDO,** although it is still common practice to leave a few pesetas for these bills also.
- Cafés serve non-alcoholic drinks and alcoholic drinks, and are normally open all day.
- You will find plates of assorted food, e.g. cheese, fish, olives, salads etc. on the bar, usually before lunchtime or dinner time. These are called **tapas,** and you can either have a portion (**una ración,** rath-yon) or food on sticks (**banderillas,** bander*ee*-yas). You have them as an apéritif or a snack with your drink. As with drinks you pay for **tapas** on leaving the bar, though some offer small **tapas** free.

WHAT TO SAY

I'd like . . . please	Quiero . . . por favor
	kee-*airo* . . . por fab-*or*
a black coffee	un café solo
	oon caf*eh* sol-o

a white coffee	**un café con leche**
	oon caf*e*h con l*e*ch-eh
a black coffee with a dash of milk	**un cortado**
	oon cort*a*d-o
a tea	**un té**
	oon t*e*h
with milk	**con leche**
	con l*e*ch-eh
with lemon	**con limón**
	con lim-*on*
a glass of milk	**un vaso de leche**
	oon b*a*sso deh l*e*ch-eh
a hot chocolate (thick)	**un chocolate**
	oon choc*o*lat-eh
a mineral water	**un agua mineral**
	oon *a*gwa miner*a*l
a lemonade	**una limonada**
	*oo*na lim-onn*a*d-ah
a Coca Cola	**una Coca Cola**
	*oo*na coca cola
an orangeade	**una naranjada**
	*oo*na na-rang-h*a*dda
an orange juice	**un zumo de naranja**
	oon th*oo*mo deh na-r*a*ng-ha
a grape juice	**un mosto**
	oon m*o*sto
a pineapple juice	**un zumo de piña**
	oon th*oo*mo deh p*i*n-ya
a milkshake	**un batido**
	oon bat*ee*do
a beer	**una cerveza**
	*oo*na thairb*e*th-ah
a draught beer	**una caña**
	*oo*na c*a*n-ya
a cider	**una sidra**
	*oo*na s*i*dra
A glass of ...	**Un vaso de ...**
	oon b*a*sso deh ...
Two glasses of ...	**Dos vasos de ...**
	dos b*a*ssos deh ...
red wine	**vino tinto**
	b*ee*no t*i*nto

Two glasses of ...	**Dos vasos de ...**
	dos bassos deh ...
white wine	**vino blanco**
	beeno blanco
rosé wine	**vino rosado**
	beeno rosad-o
claret wine	**vino clarete**
	beeno claret-eh
dry	**seco**
	sec-o
sweet	**dulce**
	dool-theh
sparkling wine	**vino espumoso**
	beeno espoomoso
champagne	**champán**
	champan
sherry	**jerez**
	herreth
A whisky	**Un whisky**
	oon whisky
with ice	**con hielo**
	con yello
with water	**con agua**
	con agwa
with soda	**con soda**
	con soda
A gin	**Una ginebra**
	oona hinnebra
and tonic	**con tonica**
	con tonica
with lemon	**con limón**
	con lim-on
A brandy/cognac	**Un coñac**
	oon con-yac
A crème de menthe	**Una crema de menta**
	oona crem-ah deh menta
A coffee liqueur	**Una crema de café**
	oona crem-ah deh cafeh
A rum	**Un ron**
	oon ron
A rum coke	**Un Cuba libre**
	oon cooba leebreh

These are local drinks you may like to try:

un anis
oon an*ee*s
aniseed liqueur, served after meals or with biscuits

un granizado
oon granecth*a*d-o
an iced drink, available in a variety of flavours

una horchata
oona orch*a*t-ah
drink made of nuts, water and sugar

una manzanilla
oona manthan*ee*-ya
similar to sherry but lighter it's an apéritif

un moscatel
oon mosca-t*el*
a sweet wine, served with desserts and sweets or biscuits

un ponche
oon p*o*nch-eh
punch, usually served after meals with the coffee

una sangria
oona sangr*ee*a
made of red wine, bitter lemon brandy and sugar – can be drunk at any time, even with meals

vino de Malaga
*bee*no deh m*a*laga
sweet wine, an apéritif

vino quinado
*bee*no kinn*a*d-o
sweet wine made of quinine – it's an appetiser

crema de cacao
cr*e*m-ah dch cac*a*-o
spirit made of cocoa, taken after meals or with the dessert

Other essential expressions:

Miss! [*This does not sound abrupt in Spanish*]
¡Señorita!
sen-yor*ee*ta

Waiter!
¡Camarero!
camma-r*airo*

The bill, please
La cuenta, por favor
la cw*e*nta por fab-*or*

How much does that come to?
¿Cuánto es?
cw*a*nto es

Is service included?
¿Está el servicio incluido?
esta el sairb*i*th-yo incloo-*ee*do

Where is the toilet, please?
¿Dónde están los servicios, por favor?
d*o*ndeh estan los sairb*i*th-yos por fab-*or*

Ordering a snack

ESSENTIAL INFORMATION

- Look for a café or bar with these signs:
  TAPAS (appetisers)
  BOCADILLOS (sandwiches)
  MERIENDAS (snacks and meals in the afternoon)
- Look for the names of snacks (listed below) on signs in the window or on the pavement.
- In some regions mobile vans sell hot snacks.
- For cakes, see p. 61.
- For ice-cream, see p. 63.
- For picnic-type snacks, see p. 68.

WHAT TO SAY

I'd like . . . please	**Quiero . . . por favor**
	kee-*air*o . . . por fab-*o*r
a cheese sandwich	**un bocadillo de queso**
	oon boccad*ee*-yo deh k*e*s-o
a ham sandwich	**un bocadillo de jamón de york**
	oon boccad*ee*-yo deh ham-*o*n deh york
a smoked ham sandwich	**un bocadillo de jamón serrano**
	oon boccad*ee*-yo deh ham-*o*n serr*a*nno

These are some other snacks you may like to try:

albondigas con tomate	spiced meatballs in tomato sauce
alb*o*ndeegas con tom*a*t-eh	
banderillas	savouries on sticks
bander*ee*-yas	
berberechos	cockles in vinegar
bairbehr*e*ch-os	
callos	tripe, usually in hot paprika sauce
c*a*-yos	
caracoles	snails
carrac*o*l-es	

empanadillas empannad*ee*-yas	small pastries with a variety of fillings
patatas bravas pat*a*t-as br*a*b-as	fried potatoes in spicy sauce
pimientos rellenos pim-yentos rel-yenos	stuffed peppers
pinchitos pinch*ee*tos	grilled kidneys or spicy sausages (usually on skewers)
tortilla de patata tort*ee*-ya deh pat*a*t-ah	Spanish omelet, made of potatoes and onions

[*For other essential expressions see 'Ordering a drink', p. 80*]

In a restaurant

ESSENTIAL INFORMATION

- The place to ask for: **un restaurante** [*see p. 17*]
- You can eat at these places:
  RESTAURANTE
  CAFETERIA (luxurious café)
  HOSTERIA
  MESON
  PARADOR   (regional cooking)
  POSADA
  ALBERGUE DE CARRETERA (roadside inn)
  FONDA (cheap simple food)
  MERENDERO (on the outskirts of a town suitable for meals or snacks during the early evening)
  CASA DE COMIDAS (a simple restaurant with typical Spanish food)
- You may also find **CASA** plus the name of the owner.
- Tipping is very common in Spain and it is usual to leave 10% of the bill for the waiter.
- By law, the menus must be displayed outside or in the window and that is the only way to judge if a place is right for your needs.
- Self-service restaurants (**AUTOSERVICIO**) are not unknown, but all other places have waiter service.
- Restaurants are usually open from 1 p.m. – 3/3.30 p.m. and from 9 p.m. – 11.30 p.m. but this can vary. It's not difficult to get a meal before 9 p.m. because lots of restaurants, especially **CASAS DE COMIDAS** or **MESONES** provide meals in the early evening (**meriendas**). And if you want to eat before 1 p.m. you can always try some **tapas** which can be a meal in themselves.
- By law, **Hojas de Reclamaciones** (Complaints Forms) must be kept in restaurants as well as in hotels, bars and petrol stations. All complaints are investigated by the Tourist Authority.

WHAT TO SAY

May I book a table?	**¿Puedo reservar una mesa?**
	pwed-o res-airbar oona mes-ah
I've booked a table	**He reservado una mesa**
	eh res-airbad-o oona mes-ah
A table ...	**Una mesa ...**
	oona mes-ah ...
for one	**para uno**
	para oono
for three	**para tres**
	para tres
The à la carte menu, please	**El menú a la carta, por favor**
	el menoo ah la carta por fab-or
The fixed-price menu	**El menú de precio fijo**
	el menoo deh preth-yo fee-ho
The (300) pesetas menu	**El menú de (trescientas) pesetas**
	el menoo deh (tres-thee-entas) pes-et-as
The tourist menu	**El menú turistico**
	el menoo touristico
Today's special menu	**El menú del día**
	el menoo del deea
The wine list	**La lista de vinos**
	la leesta deh beenos
What's this, please? [*point to menu*]	**¿Qué es eso, por favor?**
	keh es es-o por fab-or
A carafe of wine, please	**Una jarra de vino, por favor**
	oona harra deh beeno por fab-or
A quarter (25cc)	**Un cuarto**
	oon cwarto
A half (50cc)	**Medio**
	med-yo
A glass	**Un vaso**
	oon basso
A bottle	**Una botella**
	oona botel-ya
A half-bottle	**Media botella**
	med-ya botel-ya
A litre	**Un litro**
	oon litro

Red/white/rosé/house wine	**Tinto/blanco/rosado/vino de la casa**
	tinto/blanco/rosad-o/beeno deh la cas-ah
Some more bread, please	**Mas pan, por favor**
	mas pan por fab-or
Some more wine	**Mas vino**
	mas beeno
Some oil	**Aceite**
	athay-teh
Some vinegar	**Vinagre**
	beenag-reh
Some salt	**Sal**
	sal
Some pepper	**Pimienta**
	pim-yenta
Some water	**Agua**
	agwa
How much does that come to?	**¿Cuánto es?**
	cwanto es
Is service included?	**¿Está incluído el servicio?**
	esta incloo-eedo el sairbith-yo
Where is the toilet, please?	**¿Dónde está el servicio, por favor?**
	dondeh esta el sairbith-yo por fab-or
Miss! [*This does not sound abrupt in Spanish*]	**¡Señorita!**
	sen-yoreeta
Waiter!	**¡Camarero!**
	camma-rairo
The bill, please	**La cuenta, por favor**
	la cwenta por fab-or

Key words for courses, as seen on some menus:
[*Only ask this question if you want the waiter to remind you of the choice.*]

What have you got in the way of ...	**¿Qué tienen de ...**
	keh tee-en-en deh ...
STARTERS?	**ENTREMESES?**
	entreh-mess-es
SOUP?	**SOPAS?**
	sopas

EGG DISHES?	**HUEVOS?**
	web-os
FISH?	**PESCADOS?**
	pescad-os
MEAT?	**CARNES?**
	carnes
GAME?	**CAZA?**
	catha
FOWL?	**AVES?**
	abes
VEGETABLES?	**VERDURAS/LEGUMBRES?**
	bairdoo-ras/leh-goom-bres
CHEESE?	**QUESOS?**
	kes-os
FRUIT?	**FRUTAS?**
	frootas
ICE-CREAM?	**HELADOS?**
	eladdos
DESSERT?	**POSTRES?**
	pos-tres

UNDERSTANDING THE MENU

* You will find the names of the principal ingredients of most dishes on these pages:

Starters p. 69	Fruit p. 71
Meat p. 74	Cheese p. 70
Fish p. 78	Ice-cream p. 63
Vegetables p. 72	Dessert p. 61

* Used together with the following lists of cooking and menu terms, they should help you to decode the menu.
* These cooking and menu terms are for understanding only, not for speaking aloud.

Cooking and menu terms

con aceite	in oil
en adobo	marinated in red wine
al ajillo	in garlic sauce
con ajolio (allioli)	in garlic mayonnaise

ahumado	smoked
en almíbar	in syrup
asado (al ast)	roasted
a la barbacoa	barbecued
a la brasa	grilled on an open fire
en cacerola	casserole
caldo	stock
caliente	hot
cocido	boiled
crudo	raw
a la chilindrón	with tomatoes, peppers and onion
dulce	sweet
en dulce	in sweet sauce
duro	hard boiled
empanado	fried in breadcrumbs
en escabeche	marinated
escalfado	poached
estofado	braised/stewed
flameado	flamed
a la francesa	with milk, flour and butter
frio	cold
frito	fried
gratinado	browned with breadcrumbs or cheese
guisado	stewed
hervido	boiled
horneado	baked
al horno	baked
al jerez	in sherry
en su jugo	pot roasted
con mantequilla	with butter
marinado (a la marinera)	marinated
al minuto	prepared in a very short time
a la parrilla	grilled
pasado por agua	soft boiled
con perejil	with parsley
a la pescadora	with egg, lemon, wine and vinegar
a la plancha	grilled
rehogado	fried in oil with garlic and vinegar
relleno	stuffed
a la romana	deep fried
salado	salted

en salazón	cured
en salsa	in a sauce
en salsa blanca	in a white sauce
salsa mahonesa	in a mayonnaise sauce
salsa verde	sauce made from white wine, herbs, onion and flour
salsa vinagreta	sauce made from salt, vinegar and oil
salteado	sautéed
tostado	toasted
trufado	stuffed with truffles
al vapor	steamed
a la vasca	with asparagus, peas, egg, herbs, garlic, onion and flour
en vinagre	in vinegar

Further words to help you understand the menu:

anguilas	eels
arroz a la cubana	rice, fried eggs, bananas and tomato sauce
arroz a la milanesa	rice with 'chorizo' (spicy sausage), ham, cheese and peas
atún	tuna
brazo de gitano	cake filled with cream or marmalade
buñuelos (buñuelitos)	small fritters with a variety of fillings
cabeza (de cordero)	lamb's head
caldereta	fish or lamb stew
callos (a la madrileña)	tripe in piquant sauce
cocido (madrileño)	vegetable and meat stew with beans or chick-peas
codorniz	quail
cochinillo asado	suckling pig, roasted
congrio	conger eel
conejo a la aragonesa	rabbit cooked with onion, garlic, almonds and herbs
consomé	clear soup
criadillas	sweetbreads
cuajada	coagulated milk, similar to yogurt

empanada gallega	tenderloin of pork, onions and chilli pepper as filling
fabada	beans, black pudding, ham, pig's ear, onion and garlic in a stew
flan	cream caramel
gallina en pepitoria	chicken casserole with almonds and saffron
ganso	goose
garbanzos	chick-peas
gazpacho	cold spicy soup made of onion, tomatoes, peppers, bread, garlic, oil and vinegar
huevos a la flamenca	eggs baked with tomato, ham, onion, asparagus and peppers
huevos al plato	fried eggs
huevos revueltos	scrambled eggs
lentejas	lentils
lengua aragonesa	tongue with vegetables
liebre	hare
lomo	loin
magras con tomate	smoked ham fried with tomatoes
menestra (de verduras, de carne o pollo)	mixed vegetable, or meat, or chicken stew
mero (lubina)	sea bass
migas	bits of bread fried with garlic, spicy sausages, bacon and ham
natillas	custard
paella catalana	spicy pork sausages, pork, squid, tomato, chilli pepper and peas
paella marinera	fish and seafood only
paella valenciana	the classic paella with chicken, mussels, shrimp, prawns, peas, tomato, peppers and garlic
parrillada	boned and shelled fish, shellfish, chicken and meat, fried
pastel de carne	meat pie
pato	duck
pavo	turkey
perdiz	partridge
pimientos a la riojana	sweet peppers stuffed with minced meat
pisto	fried mixed vegetables

pollo a la chilindrón	chicken fried with tomatoes, peppers and smoked ham or bacon
potaje	vegetable stew
pote gallego	beans, meat, potatoes and cabbage
puchero de gallina	stewed chicken
salmonete	red mullet
sesos	brains (of lamb)
solomillo	tenderloin steak (of pork)
sopa Juliana	shredded vegetable soup
ternasco a la aragonesa	young lamb roasted with potatoes and garlic
tocino	bacon
toro de lidia	beef from the bullring
torrijas	bread soaked in milk and egg and then fried, sprinkled with sugar (french toast)
tortilla francesa	plain omelet
tortilla de patatas/española	typical Spanish omelet made with potatoes
trucha a la navarra	trout filled with smoked ham
zarzuela	savoury stew of assorted fish and shellfish

Health

ESSENTIAL INFORMATION

- There are no reciprocal health agreements between the UK and Spain. It's advisable therefore to arrange medical insurance before you travel abroad either through your travel agent, a broker or a motoring organization.
- Take your own 'first line' first aid kit with you.
- For minor disorders, and treatment at a chemist's, see p. 40.
- For finding your way to a doctor, dentist or chemist's, see p. 17.
- In case of sudden illness or an accident, you can go to a **CASA DE SOCORRO.** These are emergency first aid centres open to the general public and are free. If you have a serious accident, the same free service is provided by an **equipo quirurgico.** If you are on the road there are **PUESTOS DE SOCORRO** (first aid centres) run by the **CRUZ ROJA** (Red Cross).
- It's sometimes difficult to get an ambulance. In an emergency you are legally entitled to drive at speed, sounding your horn and waving a white handkerchief, to the nearest hospital or first aid centre: other vehicles are required by law to give way to you. If you do not have a car, wave down a motorist.
- Once in Spain, decide a definite plan of action in case of serious illness: communicate your problem to a near neighbour, the receptionist or someone you see regularly. You are then dependent on that person helping you obtain treatment.
- To find a doctor in an emergency, look for:
Médicos (in the Yellow Pages of the telephone directory)
Urgencias (Casualty department)

Casas de Socorro
Puestos de Socorro] (First aid centres)

H
Hospital] (Hospital)

What's the matter?

I have a pain in my ...	Me duele ...
	meh dwel-eh ...
abdomen	**el abdomen**
	el abdomen
ankle	**el tobillo**
	el tobee-yo
arm	**el brazo**
	el brath-o
back	**la espalda**
	la espalda
bladder	**la vejiga**
	la behee-ga
bowels	**el vientre**
	el bee-entreh
breast/chest	**el pecho**
	el pech-o
ear	**el oído**
	el oy-eedo
eye	**el ojo**
	el o-ho
foot	**el pie**
	el pee-eh
head	**la cabeza**
	la cabbeth-ah
heel	**el talón**
	el talon
jaw	**la mandíbula**
	la mandíboola
kidney	**el riñon**
	el rin-yon
leg	**la pierna**
	la pee-airna
lung	**el pulmón**
	el poolmon
neck	**el cuello**
	el cwel-yo
penis	**el pene**
	el pen-eh
shoulder	**el hombro**
	el ombro
stomach	**el estómago**
	el estommago

I have a pain in my ...	**Me duele ...**
	meh dwel-eh ...
testicle	**el testículo**
	el testicoolo
throat	**la garganta**
	la garganta
vagina	**la vagina**
	la ba-heena
wrist	**la muñeca**
	la moon-yek-ah
I have a pain here [*point*]	**Me duele aquí**
	meh dwel-eh ak-ee
I have a toothache	**Me duelen las muelas**
	meh dwel-en las mwel-as
I have broken ...	**Me he roto ...**
	meh eh rot-o ...
my dentures	**la dentadura**
	la dentadoora
my glasses	**las gafas**
	las gaf-as
I have lost ...	**He perdido ...**
	eh pairdeedo ...
my contact lenses	**mis lentes de contacto**
	mees lent-es deh contacto
a filling	**un empaste**
	oon empasteh
My child is ill	**Mi hijo/a está enfermo a***
	mee eeho/ah esta enfairmo/ah
He/she has a pain in his/her ...	**Le duele ...**
	leh dwel-eh ...
ankle [*see list above*]	**el tobillo**
	el tobee-yo

How bad is it?

I'm ill	**Estoy enfermo/a***
	estoy enfairmo/ah
It's urgent	**Es urgente**
	es oor-henteh
It's serious	**Es grave**
	es grab-eh
It's not serious	**No es grave**
	no es grab-eh

* For boys use 'o', for girls use 'a'.

It hurts	**Me duele**
	meh dwel-eh
It hurts a lot	**Me duele mucho**
	meh dwel-eh moocho
It doesn't hurt much	**No me duele mucho**
	no meh dwel-eh moocho
The pain occurs ...	**El dolor ocurre ...**
	el dol-or ocoo-reh ...
every quarter of an hour	**cada cuarto de hora**
	cad-ah cwarto deh ora
every half hour	**cada media hora**
	cad-ah med-ya ora
every hour	**cada hora**
	cad-ah ora
every day	**cada día**
	cad-ah deea
It hurts most of the time	**Me duele casi todo el tiempo**
	meh dwel-eh cas-ee tod-o el
	tee-empo
I've had it for ...	**Lo tengo desde hace ...**
	lo tengo desdeh ath-eh ...
one hour/one day	**una hora/un día**
	oona ora/oon deea
two hours/two days	**dos horas/dos días**
	dos oras/dos deeas
It's a ...	**Es un ...**
	es oon ...
sharp pain	**dolor agudo**
	dol-or agoodo
dull ache	**dolor sordo**
	dol-or sordo
nagging pain	**dolor continuo**
	dol-or contin-wo
I feel ...	**Me siento ...**
	meh see-ento ...
dizzy	**mareado**
	marreh-ad-o
sick	**mareado (con nauseas)**
	marreh-ad-o (con nows-yas)
weak	**débil**
	deb-eel
feverish	**con fiebre**
	con fee-eb-reh

Already under treatment for something else?

I take . . . regularly [*show*]	**Tomo . . . regularmente** tom-o . . . regoolarmenteh
this medicine	**esta medicina** esta meditheena
these pills	**estas píldoras** estas píldor-as
I have . . .	**Tengo . . .** tengo . . .
haemorrhoids	**hemorroides** emmoro-eed-es
rheumatism	**reuma** reh-ooma
I am . . .	**Soy . . .** soy . . .
diabetic	**diabético/a*** dee-abet-eeco/ah
asthmatic	**asmático/a*** asmatico/ah
I am allergic to (penicillin)	**Soy alérgico/a a (la penicilina)*** soy alair-heeco/ah ah (la penni-thileena)
I am pregnant	**Estoy embarazada** estoy embarrathad-ah
I have a heart condition	**Estoy del corazón** estoy del corathon

Other essential expressions

Please can you help?	**Por favor, ¿puede ayudar?** por fab-or pwed-eh a-yoodar
A doctor, please	**Un doctor, por favor** un doctor por fab-or
A dentist	**Un dentista** oon dentista
I don't speak Spanish	**No hablo español** no ablo espan-yol

* Men use 'o', women use 'a'.

What time does ... arrive?	¿A qué hora llega ... ah keh ora yeg-ah ...
the doctor	el doctor? el doctor
the dentist	el dentista? el dentista

From the doctor: key sentences to understand

Take this ...	Tome esto ... tom-eh esto ...
every day	cada día cad-ah deea
every hour	cada hora cad-ah ora
twice/four times a day	dos/cuatro veces al día dos/cwatro beth-es al deea
Stay in bed	Guarde cama gwar-deh cama
Don't travel	No viaje no bee-ah-hch
for ... days/weeks	hasta dentro de ... días/semanas asta dentro deh ... deeas/sem-annas
You must go to hospital	Tiene que ir al hospital tee-en-eh keh eer al ospital

Problems: complaints, loss, theft

ESSENTIAL INFORMATION

- Problems with
  camping facilities, see p. 34   health, see p. 94
  household appliances, see p. 52   the car, see p. 110
- If the worst comes to the worst, find the police station. To ask the way, see p. 17
- Look for:
  COMISARIA DE POLICIA (police station)
  CUARTEL DE LA GUARDIA CIVIL
  (Civil Guard – in small towns and villages)
  OFICINA DE OBJETOS PERDIDOS (lost property office)
- If you lose your passport, go to the nearest British Consulate.
- In an emergency dial 091 for the police. The numbers for Fire and Ambulance differ according to region. Remember, however, that the ambulance service is not free and nor are emergency calls from public phones.

COMPLAINTS

I bought this ...	**Compré esto ...**
	compr*eh* esto ...
today	**hoy**
	oy
yesterday	**ayer**
	a-y*air*
on Monday [see p.135]	**el lunes**
	el l*oon*-es
It's no good	**No está bien**
	no est*a* bee-*en*
Look	**Mire**
	m*ee*-reh
Here [point]	**Aquí**
	ak-*ee*
Can you ...	**¿Puede ...**
	pwed-eh ...
change it?	**cambiarlo?**
	camb-y*a*rlo

give me a refund?	**devolverme el dinero?**
	debolb*air*meh el din-*air*o
mend it?	**arreglarlo?**
	arreglar-lo
Here's the receipt	**Aquí está el recibo**
	ak-*ee* esta el reth*ee*bo
Can I see the manager?	**¿Puedo ver al director?**
	pwed-o b*air* al dirrector

LOSS

[*See also 'Theft' below; the lists are interchangeable*]

I have lost ...	**He perdido ...**
	eh paird*ee*do ...
my bag	**mi bolso**
	mee b*o*lso
my bracelet	**mi pulsera**
	mee pool*sair*a
my camera	**mi cámara**
	mee c*a*mara
my car keys	**las llaves de mi coche**
	las y*a*b-cs deh mee coch-ch
my car logbook	**mi cartilla de propriedad**
	mee cart*ee*-ya deh prop-yed-*a*d
my driving licence	**mi carnet de conducir**
	mee carnet deh condooth*ee*r
my insurance certificate	**mi certificado del seguro**
	mee thair-tificad-o del seg*oo*-ro
my jewellery	**mi joyas**
	mees h*o*y-as
everything	**todo**
	t*o*d-o

THEFT

[*See also 'Loss' above; the lists are interchangeable*]

Someone has stolen ...	**Alguien ha robado ...**
	*a*lg-yen ah robb*a*d-o ...
my car	**mi coche**
	mee c*o*ch-eh
my car radio	**la radio de mi coche**
	la r*a*d-yo deh mee c*o*ch-eh

Someone has stolen ...	**Alguien ha robado ...**
	alg-yen ah robb*ad*-o ...
my keys	**mis llaves**
	mees *yab*-es
my money	**mi dinero**
	mee din-*air*o
my necklace	**mi collar**
	mee col-y*ar*
my passport	**mi pasaporte**
	mee pas-a-p*ort*eh
my radio	**mi radio**
	mee r*ad*-yo
my tickets	**mis billetes**
	mees bee-*yet*-es
my travellers' cheques	**mis cheques de viaje**
	mees ch*eck*-es deh bee-*ah*-heh
my wallet	**mi cartera**
	mee cart*air*a
my watch	**mi reloj**
	mee rel-*ok*
my luggage	**mi equipaje**
	mee ek-eep*a*-heh

LIKELY REACTIONS: key words to understand

Wait	**Espere**
	esp*air*-eh
When?	**¿Cuándo?**
	cw*ando*
Where?	**¿Dónde?**
	d*onde*h
Name?	**¿Nombre?**
	n*ombre*h
Address?	**¿Dirección?**
	dirrekth-y*on*
I can't help you?	**No puedo ayudarle**
	no pw*ed*-o a-yood*ar*leh
Nothing to do with me	**Yo no tengo nada que ver**
	yo no t*engo* n*ad*-ah keh b*air*

The post office

ESSENTIAL INFORMATION

- To find a post office, see p. 17.
- Key words to look for:
  CORREOS
  CORREOS Y TELEGRAFOS
  SERVICIO POSTAL
- For stamps look for the words:
  SELLOS or **TIMBRES**
  or **FRANQUEOS**
- It is best to buy stamps at the
  tobacconist's. Only go to the
  post office for more
  complicated transactions,
  like telegrams.
- Look for this red and yellow
  sign on the shop:
- Letter boxes (buzones) are
  yellow. Post all overseas mail
  in the opening marked
  EXTRANJERO.
- For poste restante you should show your passport at the
  counter marked **LISTA DE CORREOS** in the main post office.
  A small fee will be charged.

WHAT TO SAY

To England, please   **Para Inglaterra, por favor**
                       para ingla-terra por fab-or

[*Hand letters, cards or parcels over the counter*]

To Australia   **Para Australia**
                      para ah-oostral-ya

To the United States **Para los Estados Unidos**
                      para los estad-os ooneedos

[*For other countries, see p. 138*]

How much is . . .	**¿Cuánto es . . .** cwanto es . . .
this parcel (to Canada)?	**este paquete (para Canadá)?** este paket-eh (para canada)
a letter (to Australia)?	**una carta (para Australia)?** oona carta (para ah-oostral-ya)
a postcard (to England)?	**una postal (para Inglaterra)?** oona postal (para ingla-terra)
Airmail	**Por avión** por ab-yon
Surface mail	**Por correo ordinario** por cor-reh-o ordinaree-o
One stamp, please	**Un sello, por favor** oon sel-yo por fab-or
Two stamps	**Dos sellos** dos sel-yos
One (15 pts) stamp	**Un sello (de quince pesetas)** oon sel-yo (deh kintheh pes-et-as)
I'd like to send a telegram	**Quiero enviar un telegrama** kee-airo embee-ar oon telegramma

Telephoning

ESSENTIAL INFORMATION

- Public telephones (**cabinas telefónicas**) are metallic grey with the words **TELEFONOS** on a green background. Calls abroad can only be made from boxes marked **INTERNACIONAL.**
- To ask the way to a public telephone, see p. 17.
- To use a public telephone: insert a 50 pts coin in the slot, lift the receiver, wait for dial tone, dial 07, wait for higher tone, dial country code (UK – 44; USA – 1; Australia – 61) then dial the town/area code followed by the subscriber's number. The following coins can be used to prolong the call: 5 pts, 25 pts, 50 pts.
- To make a phone call from a café, you will have to buy a **ficha** (counter). These are sold in cafés and are used in place of coins.
- For calls to countries which cannot be dialled direct or if you have difficulties in placing a call, go to the **CENTRAL TELEFONICA (CTNE)** or **TELEFONOS** which in large towns are open twenty-four hours a day. In **la Telefonica**, the operator will put your call through and give you the bill afterwards. Just write the town and number you want on a piece of paper and hand it over to the operator. Add **de persona a persona** if you want a person-to-person call or **a cobro revertido** if you want to reverse the charges.
- In Spain the telephone network operates independently of the post office, so don't expect to find phones in post offices.
- Before travelling abroad, ask at your local post office for details of phoning England from Spain.

WHAT TO SAY

Where can I make a telephone call?

¿Dónde puedo llamar por teléfono?

dondeh pwed-o yam*a*r por tel*e*f-ono

Local/abroad

Local/al extranjero

loc*a*l/ al extran-h*a*iro

I'd like this number . . .
[*show number*]
  in England

  in Canada

  in the USA

Quiero este número . . .
kee-*airo* esteh n*oo*mairo . . .
en Inglaterra
en ingla-terra
en Canadá
en canad*a*
en los Estados Unidos
en los est*a*d-os oon*ee*dos

[*For other countries, see p. 138*]

Can you dial it for me,
  please?

How much is it?

Hello!

May I speak to . . . ?

Extension

I'm sorry, I don't speak
  Spanish
Do you speak English?

Thank you, I'll phone back

Good-bye

**¿Puede usted marcar por mí, por
favor?**
pwed-eh oosted marcar por m*ee*
por fab-*or*
¿Cuánto es?
cwanto es
¡Hola!
o-la
¿Puedo hablar con . . . ?
pwed-o abl*ar* con . . .
Extensión
extens-yon
Lo siento, no hablo español
lo see-*en*to no *a*blo espan-y*ol*
¿Habla usted inglés?
*a*bla oosted in-gles
Gracias, volveré a llamar
gr*a*th-yas bolbair-eh ah yam*ar*
Adiós
ad-y*os*

LIKELY REACTIONS

That's 80 pesetas   **Son ochenta pesetas**
son ochenta pes-*et*-as

Cabin number (3)   **Cabina número (tres)**
cab*ee*na n*oo*mairo tr*es*

[*For numbers, see p. 131*]

Don't hang up   **No cuelgue**
no cw*el*g-eh

I'm trying to connect you   **Estoy intentando comunicarle**
est*oy* intent*a*ndo comoonic*a*rleh

You're through   **Hable**
*a*b-leh

There's a delay   **Hay retraso**
*a*h-ee retr*a*s-o

I'll try again   **Probaré otra vez**
proba-r*eh* *o*t-ra beth

Changing cheques and money

ESSENTIAL INFORMATION

- Finding your way to a bank or change bureau, see p. 17.
- Look for these words:
  BANCO (bank)
  CAJA DE AHORROS (savings bank)
  CAMBIO (change)
  CAJA DE CAMBIO (cash desk in a bank)
  OFICINA DE CAMBIO (bureau de change)
- To cash your normal cheques, exactly as at home, use your banker's card where you see the Eurocheque sign. Write in English, in pounds.
- Exchange rate information might show the pound as:
  £, L, Libra Esterlina, or even **GB**.
- Have your passport handy and remember that in Spain banks open at 9 a.m. and close at 2 p.m. and on Saturdays at 1 p.m.

WHAT TO SAY

I'd like to cash . . .

   this travellers' cheque

   these travellers' cheques

   this cheque

I'd like to change this into Spanish pesetas

Here's . . .

   my banker's card

   my passport

Quiero cobrar . . .
kee-*airo* cobr*ar* . . .
este cheque de viaje
*e*steh ch*e*ck-eh deh bee-*a*h-heh
estos cheques de viaje
*e*stos ch*e*ck-es deh bee-*a*h-heh
este cheque
*e*steh ch*e*ck-eh
Quiero cambiar esto en pesetas españolas
kee-*airo* camb-y*ar* esto en pes-*e*t-as espan-y*o*las

Aquí está . . .
ak-*ee* est*a* . . .
mi tarjeta de banco
mee tarh*e*t-ah deh b*a*nco
mi pasaporte
mee pas-ap*o*rteh

For excursions into neighbouring countries:

I'd like to change this ...	**Quiero cambiar esto ...**
[*show banknotes*]	kee-*airo* camb-y*ar* esto ...
into French francs	**en francos franceses**
	en fr*anc*-os franth*es*-es
into Italian lire	**en liras italianas**
	en l*ee*-ras itali*ann*as
into Portuguese escudos	**en escudos portugueses**
	en esc*oo*dos portoog*es*-es
What is the rate of exchange?	**¿A cuánto está el cambio?**
	ah cw*anto* est*a* el c*amb*-yo

LIKELY REACTIONS

Passport, please	**Pasaporte, por favor**
	pas-ap*orte*h por fab-*or*
Sign here	**Firme aquí**
	f*eer*-meh ak-*ee*
Your banker's card, please	**Su tarjeta de banco, por favor**
	s*oo* tarh*et*-ah deh b*u*nco por fab-*or*
Go to the cash desk	**Vaya a caja**
	b*a*-ya ah c*a*-ha

Car travel

ESSENTIAL INFORMATION

- Finding a filling station or garage, see p. 17.
- Look for these signs:
  GASOLINA (petrol)
  GASOLINERA (petrol station)
  ESTACION DE SERVICIO (petrol station)
- Grades of petrol: **EXTRA** (4 star)
  NORMAL (2 star standard) **GAS-OIL** (diesel)
  SUPER (3 star)   **DOS TIEMPOS** (two stroke)
- 1 gallon is about 4½ litres (accurate enough up to 6 gallons).
- Petrol prices are standardized all over Spain, and a minimum sale of 5 litres is often imposed.
- For car repairs, look for signs with red, blue and white stripes or
  GARAJE
  TALLER DE REPARACIONES
- Most petrol stations operate a 24-hour service, though some close late at night. Take care, however, as the stations themselves are few and far between.
- Garages will open at 8 or 9 a.m. and close between 7.30 and 8 p.m. Most will close lunchtime.
- Unfamiliar road signs and warnings, see p. 125.

WHAT TO SAY

[*For numbers, see p. 131*]

(Nine) litres of ...	(Nueve) litros de ... (nweb-eh) litros deh ...
(Five hundred) pesetas of ...	(Quinientas) pesetas de ... (kin-yentas) pes-et-as deh ...
standard	normal normal
premium	super soopair
diesel	gas-oil gas-oil
Fill it up, please	Lleno, por favor yeno por fab-or

Can you check ...	**¿Puede mirar ...** pwed-eh mee-rar ...
the oil?	**el aceite?** el ath*a*y-teh
the battery?	**la batería?** la batteh-r*ee*a
the radiator?	**el radiador?** el rad-yad-*o*r
the tyres?	**los neumáticos?** los neh-oom*a*tticos
I've run out of petrol	**Me he quedado sin gasolina** meh eh ked-*a*d-o sin gasol*ee*na
Can I borrow a can, please?	**¿Puede dejarme una lata, por favor?** pwed-eh deh-h*a*rmeh *oo*na l*a*tta por fab-*o*r
My car has broken down	**Se ha averiado mi coche** se ah abbeh-ree-*a*do mee c*o*ch-eh
My car won't start	**Mi coche no arranca** mee c*o*ch-eh no arr*a*nca
I've had an accident	**He tenido un accidente** eh ten*ee*do oon ak-thee*de*nteh
I've lost my car keys	**He perdido las llaves de mi coche** eh paird*ee*do las y*a*b-es deh mee c*o*ch-eh
My car is ...	**Mi coche está ...** mee c*o*ch-eh est*a* ...
two kilometres away	**a dos kilómetros** ah dos kil*o*metros
three kilometres away	**a tres kilómetros** ah tres kil*o*metros
Can you help me, please?	**¿Puede ayudarme, por favor** pwed-eh a-yood*a*rmeh por fab-*o*r
Do you do repairs?	**¿Hacen reparaciones?** *a*th-en reparath-y*o*n-es
I have a puncture	**Tengo un neumático pinchado** tengo oon neh-oom*a*ttico pinch*a*d-o
I have a broken windscreen	**Tengo el parabrisas roto** tengo el parabr*ee*s-as r*o*t-o
I think the problem is here ... [*point*]	**Creo que el problema esta aquí ...** creh-o keh el problem-ah est*a* ak-*ee* ...
I don't know what's wrong	**No se lo que está mal** no seh lo keh est*a* mal

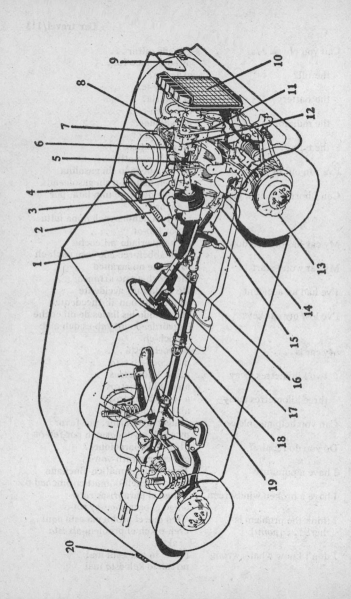

1	windscreen wipers	limpiaparabrisas limp-ya-parabree-sas
2	fuses	fusibles fooseebles
3	heater	calentador calenta-dor
4	battery	batería batteh-reea
5	engine	motor mot-or
6	fuel pump	bomba de gasolina bomba deh gasoleena
7	starter motor	motor de arranque mot-or deh arrankeh
8	carburettor	carburador carboo-rad-or
9	lights	faros faros
10	radiator	radiador rad-yad-or

11	fan belt	correa del ventilador correh-ah del bentillador
12	generator	generador henneh-rad-or
13	brakes	frenos fren-os
14	clutch	embrague embrag-eh
15	gear box	caja de cambios ca-ha de camb-yos
16	steering	dirección dirrekth-yon
17	ignition	encendido enthendeedo
18	transmission	transmisión transmis-yon
19	exhaust	tubo de escape toobo deh escap-eh
20	indicators	indicadores indic-ad-or-es

Can you ...	**¿Puede ...**
	pwed-eh ...
repair the fault?	**reparar la avería?**
	reppar*ar* la abbeh-*ree*a
come and look?	**venir a ver?**
	ben-*eer* ah b*air*
estimate the cost?	**estimar el coste?**
	estim*ar* el c*o*steh
write it down?	**escribirlo?**
	escrib-*eer*-lo
Do you accept these coupons?	**¿Aceptan estos cupones?**
	ath*e*ptan *e*stos coop*o*n-es
How long will the repair take?	**¿Cuánto tiempo tardarán en repararlo?**
	cw*a*nto tee-*e*mpo tarda-r*a*n en reppar*ar*-lo
When will the car be ready?	**¿Cuando estará listo el coche?**
	cw*a*ndo estar*a* l*i*sto el c*o*ch-eh
Can I see the bill?	**¿Puedo ver la cuenta?**
	pwed-o b*air* la cw*e*nta
This is my insurance document	**Este es mi documento del seguro**
	*e*steh es mee doc*oo*mento del seg*oo*-ro

HIRING A CAR

Can I hire a car?	**¿Puedo alquilar un coche?**
	pwed-o alkeel*ar* oon c*o*ch-eh
I need a car ...	**Necesito un coche ...**
	neth-es*ee*to oon c*o*ch-eh ...
for two people	**para dos personas**
	p*a*ra dos pairson-as
for five people	**para cinco personas**
	p*a*ra th*i*nko pairson-as
for one day	**para un día**
	p*a*ra oon d*ee*a
for five days	**para cinco días**
	p*a*ra th*i*nko d*ee*as
for a week	**para una semana**
	p*a*ra *oo*na sem-*a*nna

Can you write down ...	¿Puede escribir ...
	pwed-eh escrib-cer ...
the deposit to pay?	el depósito de pago?
	el deposit-o deh pag-o
the charge per kilometre?	el precio por kilómetro?
	el preth-yo por kilometro
the daily charge?	el precio por día?
	el preth-yo por deea
the cost of insurance?	el precio del seguro?
	el preth-yo del segoo-ro
Can I leave it in (Madrid)?	¿Puedo dejarlo en (Madrid)?
	pwed-o deh-harlo en (madrid)
What documents do I need?	¿Que documentos necesito?
	keh docoomentos neth-eseeto

LIKELY REACTIONS

We don't do repairs	No se hacen reparaciones
	no seh ath-en reparath-yon-es
Where is your car?	¿Dónde está su coche?
	dondeh esta soo coch-eh
What make is it?	¿Qué tipo es?
	keh teepo es
Come back tomorrow/on Monday	Vuelva mañana/el lunes
	bwelba manyan-ah/el loon-es

[*For days of the week, see p. 135*]

We don't hire cars	No se alquilan coches
	no seh alkeelan coch-es
Your driving licence, please	Su carnet de conducir, por favor
	soo carnet deh condoo-theer por fab-or
The mileage is unlimited	El kilometraje es ilimitado
	el kilometra-heh es illimit-ad-o

Public transport

ESSENTIAL INFORMATION

- Finding the way to a bus station, bus stop, tram stop, railway station and taxi rank, see p. 17.
- Taxis are usually black saloons with a coloured line painted along the side. They display a green light at night and during the day a sign on the windscreen which says **LIBRE** (free) if they are available.
- These are the different types of trains, graded according to speed (slowest to fastest):
  TAF/FERROBUS/OMNIBUS
  TRANVIAS/AUTOMOTOR (all short distance local trains, not very reliable)
  EXPRESO/RAPIDO (do not be misled by their names; these are both *slow* trains the only difference being the first travels by night, the second by day)
  ELECTROTREN (fast and comfortable)
  TER (fast and comfortable – supplement payable)
  TALGO (luxury train – supplement payable)
- Key words on signs [*see also p. 125*]
  ANDEN (platform)
  BILLETES (tickets, ticket office)
  CONSIGNA/EQUIPAJES (left-luggage)
  DESPACHO DE BILLETES/TAQUILLA (ticket office)
  ENTRADA (entrance)
  HORARIO (timetable)
  LLEGADA (arrival)
  OFICINA DE INFORMACION (information office)
  PARADA (bus stop, taxi stop)
  PROHIBIDO (forbidden)
  RENFE (initials of Spanish railways)
  SALIDA (exit)
- Children travel free up to the age of three and pay half-price up to the age of seven. However, if you have an international ticket, children can travel free up to the age of four and travel half-price up to the age of twelve.
- On certain dates throughout the year known as **Días Azules** (Blue Days), numerous reductions are available on train travel;

check with the Spanish Tourist Office for dates and further information.
- On buses and tubes there is a flat rate irrespective of distance and it is cheaper to buy a taco (book of tickets) for underground travel. Tubes operate between 6 a.m. and 1 a.m.
- It is worth booking train and coach journeys in advance.

WHAT TO SAY

Where does the train for (Madrid) leave from?
¿De dónde sale el tren para (Madrid)?
deh dondeh sal-eh el tren para (madrid)

At what time does the train leave for (Madrid)?
¿A qué hora sale el tren para (Madrid)?
ah keh ora sal-eh el tren para (madrid)

At what time does the train arrive in (Madrid)?
¿A qué hora llega el tren a (Madrid)?
ah keh ora yeg-ah el tren ah (madrid)

Is this the train for (Madrid)?
¿Es éste el tren para (Madrid)?
es esteh el tren para (madrid)

Where does the bus for (Barcelona) leave from?
¿De dónde sale el autobús para (Barcelona)?
deh dondeh sal-eh el ah-ooto-boos para (barthelona)

At what time does the bus leave for (Barcelona)?
¿A qué hora sale el autobús para (Barcelona)?
ah keh ora sal-eh el ah-ooto-boos para (barthelona)

At what times does the bus arrive at (Barcelona)?
¿A qué hora llega el autobús a (Barcelona)?
ah keh ora yeg-ah el ah-ooto-boos a (barthelona)

Is this the bus for (Barcelona)?
¿Es éste el autobús para (Barcelona)?
es esteh el ah-ooto-boos para (barthelona)

Do I have to change?
¿Tengo que cambiar?
tengo keh camb-yar

Where does . . . leave from?	**¿De dónde sale . . .**
	deh dondeh sal-eh . . .
the bus	**el autobús**
	el ah-ooto-boos
the boat/ferry	**el barco/ferry**
	el barco/ferree
the train	**el tren**
	el tren
the underground	**el metro**
	el metro
for the airport	**para el aeropuerto?**
	para el airo-pwairto
for the cathedral	**para la catedral?**
	para la cattedral
for the beach	**para la playa?**
	para la pla-ya
for the market place	**para el mercado?**
	para el maircad-o
for the railway station	**para la estación de tren?**
	para la estath-yon deh tren
for the town centre	**para el centro de la ciudad?**
	para el thentro deh la thee-oodad
for the town hall	**para el ayuntamiento?**
	para el a-yoontam-yento
for St John's church	**para la iglesia de San Juan?**
	para la eegles-ya deh san hwan
for the swimming pool	**para la piscina?**
	para la pis-theena
Is this . . .	**¿Es éste . . .**
	es esteh . . .
the bus for the market place?	**el autobús para el mercado?**
	el ah-ooto-boos para el maircad-o
the tram for the railway station?	**el tranvía para la estación de tren?**
	el trambeea para la estath-yon deh tren
Where can I get a taxi?	**¿Dónde puedo tomar un taxi?**
	dondeh pwed-o tom-ar oon taxi
Can you put me off at the right stop, please?	**¿Puede avisarme en mi parada, por favor?**
	pwed-eh absee-sarmeh en mee parad-ah por fab-or
Can I book a seat?	**¿Puedo reservar un asiento?**
	pwed-o res-airbar oon as-yento

A single	**Un billete de ida solamente** oon bee-yet-eh deh *ee*da solamenteh
A return	**Un billete de ida y vuelta** oon bee-yet-eh deh *ee*da ee bwelta
First class	**Primera clase** prim-*air*a classeh
Second class	**Segunda clase** seg-*oo*nda classeh
One adult	**Un adulto** oon ad*oo*lto
Two adults	**Dos adultos** dos ad*oo*ltos
and one child	**y un niño** ee oon neen-yo
and two children	**y dos niños** ee dos neen-yos
How much is it?	**¿Cuánto es?** cwanto es

LIKELY REACTIONS

Over there	**Allí** ay*ee*
Here	**Aquí** ak-*ee*
Platform (1)	**Andén (primero)** anden (prim-*air*o)
At (four o'clock) [*For times, see p. 133*]	**A las (cuatro)** ah las (cwatro)
Change at (Zaragoza)	**Cambie en (Zaragoza)** camb-yeh en (tharragotha)
Change at (the town hall)	**Cambie en (el ayuntamiento)** camb-yeh en (el a-yoontam-y*en*to)
This is your stop	**Esta es su parada** esta es soo parad-ah
There is only first class	**Sólo hay primera clase** solo ah-ee prim-*air*a classeh
There is a supplement	**Hay un suplemento** ah-ee oon sooplem*en*to

Leisure

ESSENTIAL INFORMATION

- Finding the way to a place of entertainment, see p. 17.
- For times of day, see p. 133.
- Important signs, see p. 125.
- It is quite normal for most shows, films or plays, to have a late night session and for the performance to end at 1 or 2 a.m.
- Smoking is strictly forbidden in cinemas and theatres. You should tip the ushers or usherettes (a few pesetas).
- Most cinema and theatre seats can be booked in advance.
- In bars, cafés and restaurants it is customary to leave a tip, even if you drink at the counter; and you pay when you leave.

WHAT TO SAY

At what times does . . . open?	¿A qué hora abre . . .
	ah keh ora ab-reh . . .
the art gallery	la galería de arte?
	la gal-ereea deh art-eh
the botanical garden	el jardín botánico?
	el hardeen botanic-o
the cinema	el cine?
	el thin-eh
the concert hall	la sala de conciertos?
	la sal-ah deh conth-yairtos
the disco	la discoteca?
	la discotec-ah
the museum	el museo?
	el moo-sey-o
the nightclub	la sala de fiestas?
	la sal-ah deh fee-estas
the sports stadium	el estadio de deportes?
	el estad-yo deh dep-ort-es
the swimming pool	la piscina?
	la pis-theena
the theatre	el teatro?
	el teh-atro
the zoo	el zoo?
	el thoh-o

At what time does . . . close?   **¿A qué hora cierra . . .**
ah keh ora thee-erra . . .

   the art gallery   **la galería de arte?**
la gal-ereea deh art-eh

[see above list]

At what time does . . . start?   **¿A qué hora empieza . . .**
ah keh ora emp-yeth-ah . . .

   the cabaret   **el cabaret?**
el cabaret

   the concert   **el concierto?**
el conth-yairto

   the film   **la película?**
la pelicoo-la

   the match   **el partido?**
el parteedo

   the play   **la obra?**
la obra

   the race   **la carrera?**
la carraira

How much is it . . .   **¿Cuánto es . . .**
cwanto es . . .

   for an adult?   **por un adulto?**
por oon adoolto

   for a child?   **por un niño?**
por oon neen-yo

Two adults, please   **Dos adultos, por favor**
dos adooltos por fab-or

Three children, please   **Tres niños, por favor**
tres neen-yos por fab-or

[State price, if there's a choice]

Stalls/circle/sun/shade   **Butaca/anfiteatro/sol/sombra**
bootac-ah/anfee-teh-atro/sol/
sombra

Do you have . . .   **¿Tiene . . .**
tee-en-eh . . .

   a programme?   **un programa?**
oon programma

   a guide book?   **una guía?**
oona gheea

Where's the toilet, please?   **¿Dónde están los servicios, por favor?**
dondeh estan los sairbith-yos por fab-or

Where's the cloakroom?	¿Dónde está el guardarropa?
	dondeh esta el gwarda-ropa
I would like lessons in . . .	Quiero lecciones de . . .
	kee-airo lekth-yon-es deh . . .
skiing	esquí
	eskee
sailing	vela
	bel-ah
water skiing	esquí acuático
	eskee aquatic-o
sub-aqua diving	buceo
	bootheh-o
Can I hire . . .	¿Puedo alquilar . . .
	pwed-o alkeelar . . .
some skis?	unos esquís?
	oonos eskees
some skiboots?	unas botas de esquí?
	oonas bot-as deh eskee
a boat?	un bote?
	oon bot-eh
a fishing rod?	una caña de pescar?
	oona can-ya deh pescar
a deck-chair?	una hamaca?
	oona amacca
a sun umbrella?	una sombrilla?
	oona sombree-ya
the necessary equipment?	el equipo necesario?
	el ekeepo nethesarrio
How much is it . . .	¿Cuánto es . . .
	cwanto es . . .
per day/per hour?	por día/por hora?
	por deea/por ora
Do I need a licence?	¿Necesito licencia?
	neth-eseeto leethenth-ya

Asking if things are allowed

ESSENTIAL INFORMATION

- May one smoke here?
  May we smoke here?
  May I smoke here?
  Can one smoke here?   ¿Se puede fumar aquí?
  Can we smoke here?
  Can I smoke here?
- All these English variations can be expressed in one way in Spanish. To save space, only the first English version (May one . . . ?) is shown below.

WHAT TO SAY

Excuse me, please	**Perdone, por favor**
	paird*on*-eh por fab-*or*
May one . . .	**¿Se puede . . .**
	seh pw*ed*-eh . . .
camp here?	**acampar aquí?**
	ac*a*mp*ar* ak-*ee*
come in?	**entrar?**
	entr*ar*
dance here?	**bailar aquí?**
	by-l*ar* ak-*ee*
fish here?	**pescar aquí?**
	pesc*ar* ak-*ee*
get a drink here?	**obtener una bebida aquí?**
	obten-*air* *oo*na bebeeda ak-*ee*
get out this way?	**salir por aquí?**
	sal*ee*r por ak-*ee*
get something to eat here?	**obtener algo de comer?**
	obten-*air* algo deh com-*air*
leave one's things here?	**dejar las cosas aquí?**
	deh-h*ar* las c*os*-as ak-*ee*
look around?	**mirar esto?**
	mee-r*ar* esto
park here?	**aparcar aquí?**
	aparc*ar* ak-*ee*

May one . . .	¿Se puede . . .
	seh pwed-eh . . .
picnic here?	comer aquí?
	com-air ak-ee
sit here?	sentar aquí?
	sentar ak-ee
smoke here?	fumar aquí?
	foomar ak-ee
swim here?	nadar aquí?
	nad-ar ak-ee
take photos here?	tomar fotos aquí?
	tom-ar fotos ak-ee
telephone here?	telefonear aquí?
	telefoneh-ar ak-ee
wait here?	esperar aquí?
	esperar ak-ee

LIKELY REACTIONS

Yes, certainly	Sí, desde luego
	see desdeh lweg-o
Help yourself	Sírvase usted mismo
	seerba-seh oosted mismo
I think so	Creo que sí
	creh-o keh see
Of course	Claro
	clar-o
Yes, but be careful	Sí, pero tenga cuidado
	see perro tenga cweedad-o
No, certainly not	No, desde luego que no
	no desdeh lweg-o keh no
I don't think so	No creo
	no creh-o
Not normally	Normalmente no
	normalmenteh no
Sorry	Lo siento
	lo see-ento

Reference

PUBLIC NOTICES

● Key words on signs for drivers, pedestrians, travellers, shoppers and overnight guests.

ABIERTO	Open
ADUANA	Customs
AGUA POTABLE	Drinking water
ALQUILER DE COCHES	Cars for hire
ALTO	Halt
ANDEN	Platform
APARCAMIENTO	Car park
ASCENSOR	Lift
ASEOS	Toilets
ATENCION AL TREN	Beware of the trains
AUTOBUS SOLAMENTE	For buses (only)
AUTOPISTA	Motorway
AUTOSERVICIO	Self-service
BADEN PERMANENTE	In constant use (no parking)
BAR	Bar
BAÑOS	Baths
CABALLEROS	Gentlemen
CAJA	Cash desk
CALIENTE	Hot (tap)
CALZADA DETERIORADA	Bad surface
CALLEJON SIN SALIDA	Cul-de-sac
CAMINO CERRADO	Road closed
CAÑADA	Cattle crossing
CAZA	Hunting
CEDA EL PASO	Give way
CENTRO CIUDAD	Town centre
CERRADO	Closed
CERRADO POR VACACIONES	Closed for holiday period
CIRCULACION EN AMBAS DIRECCIONES	Two-way traffic
CIRCULEN POR LA DERECHA	Keep right

COCHE-RESTAURANTE	Dining car
COMEDOR	Dining room
COMPLETO	No vacancies
CONSERJE	Porter
CONSIGNA	Left luggage
CRUCE	Crossroads
CRUCE DE CICLISTAS	Cycle crossing
CRUCE DE BAÑO	Bathroom
CUIDADO	Watch out
CUIDADO CON EL PERRO	Beware of the dog
CURVA PELIGROSA	Dangerous bend
DAMAS	Ladies
DESPACIO	Drive slowly
DESPACHO DE BILLETES	Ticket office
DESPRENDIMIENTO DEL TERRENO	Falling stones
DESVIO	Diversion
DIRECCION UNICA	One-way (street)
DISCO OBLIGATORIO	Parking discs required
DUCHA	Shower
EMPUJE	Push
ENCIENDA LOS FAROS	Lights on
ENTRADA	Entrance
ENTRADA LIBRE	Admission/Entrance free
ENTRE SIN LLAMAR	Come in without knocking
ES PELIGROSO ASOMARSE AL EXTERIOR	It's dangerous to lean out of the window
ESCALERA AUTOMATICA	Escalator
ESCUELA	School
ESPERE	Wait
ESTACIONAMIENTO LIMITADO	Restricted parking
ESTRECHAMIENTO DE CALZADA	Road narrows
FINAL DE AUTOPISTA	End (motorway)
FIRME (SUPERFICIE) DESLIZANTE	Slippery surface (road)
FRIO	Cold
GUIA	Guide
HORAS DE VISITA	Visiting hours

INFORMACION	Information office/desk
JORNADA INTENSIVA	Shop opens early in the morning and closes in the afternoon (e.g. 8 a.m. – 2 p.m.)
LAVABOS	Lavatories
LIQUIDACION	Sale
LLAME A LA PUERTA	Knock (door)
LLAME AL TIMBRE	Ring (bell)
LLEGADAS	Arrivals
MAYORES	Adults
METRO	Underground (train)
NIÑOS	Children
NO HAY ENTRADAS (LOCALIDADES)	House full (cinema, theatre etc)
NO POTABLE	Not for drinking
NO SE ADMITEN CARAVANAS	No caravans
NO TOCAR	Do not touch
OBJETOS PERDIDOS	Lost property
OBRAS	Road works
OCUPADO	Occupied
OFERTA ESPECIAL	Special offer
OJO AL TREN	Beware of the trains
PARADA	Stop
PASEN	Cross (the road)
PASO A NIVEL	Level crossing
PASO SUBTERRANEO	Subway
PEAJE	Toll
PEATON, CIRCULA POR TU IZQUIERDA	Pedestrian keep to the left
PEATONES	Pedestrians
PELIGRO	Danger
PELIGRO DE INCENDIO	Danger of fire
PESCA	Fishing
PISO (PRIMERO, SEGUNDO, TERCERO, PLANTA BAJA SOTANO	Floor (first, second, third, ground, basement)
PLAZAS LIBRES	Vacancies
POLICIA	Police
PRECAUCION	Caution
PRECIOS FIJOS	Fixed prices

PRINCIPIO DE AUTOPISTA	Start (of motorway)
PRIORIDAD A LA DERECHA	Priority to the right
PRIVADO	Private
PROHIBIDO	Forbidden
PROHIBIDO ADELANTAR	Overtaking forbidden
PROHIBIDO APARCAR	No parking
PROHIBIDO BAÑARSE SIN GORRO	No bathing without a cap
PROHIBIDO EL PASO	Trespassers will be prosecuted
PROHIBIDO FUMAR	No smoking
PROHIBIDO HABLAR AL CONDUCTOR	No talking to the driver
PROHIBIDO HACER CAMPING	No camping
PROHIBIDO PISAR EL CESPED	Keep off the grass
PROHIBIDO TOMAR FOTOGRAFIAS	No photographs
REBAJAS	Sales
RECIEN PINTADO	Wet paint
RECEPCION	Reception
REDUZCA VELOCIDAD	Slow down
RESERVADO	Reserved
RESERVAS	Reservations
RETRETE	Toilets
SALA DE ESPERA	Waiting room
SALDOS	Sales
SALIDA	Exit
SALIDA DE EMERGENCIA	Emergency exit
SALIDAS	Departures
SE ALQUILA HABITACION	Room for rent
SE PROHIBE LA ENTRADA	No admission/no entry
SE VENDE	For sale
SEMAFORO	Traffic lights
SEÑORAS	Ladies
SEÑORES	Gentlemen
SERVICIOS	Toilets
SIGA ADELANTE	Go

SILENCIO	Quiet
TAQUILLA	Ticket office
VEHICULOS PESADOS	For heavy vehicles
VELOCIDAD LIMITADA	Speed limit
VENENO	Poison
VENTA	For sale
VENTANILLA	Window (of booking office)
ZONA AZUL	Restricted parking
ZONA DE AVALANCHAS	Avalanche area

ABBREVIATIONS

A	**Albergue**	inn/hostel
ANCE	**Agrupación Nacional de campings de España**	Spanish Federation of Camping Sites
apdo	**apartado (de correos)**	post office box
Av/Avda	**Avenida**	avenue
C	**Carretera comarcal**	provincial road
	Caliente	hot (water tap)
C/	**Calle**	street
	Cuenta	account
CAMPSA	**Compañía Arrendataria del Monopolio de petróleos Sociedad Anónima**	National petrol company
cént(s)	**céntimo(s)**	hundredth part of a peseta
CN	**Carretera Nacional**	national road
CT	**Centro Turístico**	tourist centre
CTNE	**Compañia Telefónica Nacional de España**	Spanish Telephone company
dcha	**derecha**	right
do	**descuento**	discount
F	**Frío**	cold (water tap)
FC	**Ferrocarril**	railway
FEVE	**Ferrocarriles Españoles de Via Estrecha**	Spanish railway company
GC	**Guardia Civil**	Civil Guard
h	**hora**	hour
	habitantes	inhabitants
	hacia	circa
IB	**Iberia**	Spanish aviation company

izq	izquierdo	left
km/h	kilómetros por hora	kilometres per hour
kv	kilovatios	kilowatts
L	Carretera Local	local road
	Libra	English pound
Lleg	Llegadas	Arrivals
MIT	Ministerio de Información y Turismo	Ministry of Tourism
N	Nacional (carretera)	national road
	norte	north
n° num.]	número	number
NO	noroeste	northwest
OP	Obras Públicas	Public Works
P°	Paseo	avenue
pta(s)	peseta(s)	peseta(s)
PVP	Precio de Venta al Público	Sale price to the public
RACE	Real Automóvil Club de España	Royal Automobile Club of Spain
REAJ	Red Española de Albergues Juveniles	Youth Hostel Association
RENFE	Red Nacional de Ferrocarriles Españoles	Spanish national railway company
Sal	Salidas	Departures
Sr	Señor	Mr
Sra	Señora	Mrs
Sres	Señores	Messrs
Srta	Señorita	Miss
SP	Servicio Público	Public Service (taxis and buses)
SR	Sin Reserva	without reservation
Tfno	Teléfono	Telephone
TVE	Televisión Española	Spanish television company
Vda de	viuda de	widow of
vg, vgr	verbigracia	namely

NUMBERS

Cardinal numbers

0	cero	thairo
1	uno	oono
2	dos	dos
3	tres	tres
4	cuatro	cwatro
5	cinco	thinko
6	seis	seys
7	siete	see-et-eh
8	ocho	ocho
9	nueve	nweb-eh
10	diez	dee-eth
11	once	ontheh
12	doce	doth-eh
13	trece	treth-ch
14	catorce	cat-ortheh
15	quince	kintheh
16	dieciséis	dee-ethee-seys
17	diecisiete	dee-ethee-see-et-eh
18	dieciocho	dee-ethee-ocho
19	diecinueve	dee-ethee-nweb-eh
20	veinte	beynteh
21	veintiuno	beyntee-oono
22	veintidós	beyntee-dos
23	veintitrés	beyntee-tres
24	veinticuatro	beyntee-cwatro
25	veinticinco	beyntee-thinko
26	veintiséis	beyntee-seys
27	veintisiete	beyntee-see-et-eh
28	veintiocho	beyntee-ocho
29	veintinueve	beyntee-nweb-eh
30	treinta	treynta
31	treinta y uno	treynta ee oono
35	treinta y cinco	treynta ee thinko
38	treinta y ocho	treynta ee ocho
40	cuarenta	cwa-renta
41	cuarenta y uno	cwa-renta ee oono
45	cuarenta y cinco	cwa-renta ee thinko
48	cuarenta y ocho	cwa-renta ee ocho

50	cincuenta	thin-cwenta
55	cincuenta y cinco	thin-cwenta ee thinko
60	sesenta	ses-enta
65	sesenta y cinco	ses-enta ee thinko
70	setenta	set-enta
75	setenta y cinco	set-enta ee thinko
80	ochenta	ochenta
85	ochenta y cinco	ochenta ee thinko
90	noventa	nobenta
95	noventa y cinco	nobenta ee thinko
100	cien	thee-en
101	ciento uno	thee-ento oono
102	ciento dos	thee-ento dos
125	ciento veinticinco	thee-ento beyntee-thinko
150	ciento cincuenta	thee-ento thin-cwenta
175	ciento setenta y cinco	thee-ento set-enta ee thinko
200	doscientos	dos-thee-entos
300	trescientos	tres-thee-entos
400	cuatrocientos	cwatro-thee-entos
500	quinientos	kin-yentos
1000	mil	mil
1500	mil quinientos	mil kin-yentos
2000	dos mil	dos mil
5000	cinco mil	thinko mil
10,000	diez mil	dee-eth mil
100,000	cien mil	thee-en mil
1,000,000	un millón	oon mil-yon

Ordinal numbers

1st	primero (1°)	prim-airo
2nd	segundo (2°)	se-goondo
3rd	tercero (3°)	tair-thairo
4th	cuarto (4°)	cwarto
5th	quinto (5°)	kinto
6th	sexto (6°)	sexto
7th	séptimo (7°)	septeemo
8th	octavo (8°)	octabo-o
9th	noveno (9°)	nob-en-o
10th	décimo (10°)	deth-eemo
11th	undécimo onceno	undeth-eemo onth-eno
12th	duodécimo	doo-odeth-eemo

TIME

What time is it?	**¿Qué hora es?**
	keh *ora es*
It's one o'clock	**Es la una**
	es la *oo*na
It's ...	**Son ...**
	son ...
two o'clock	**las dos**
	las d*os*
three o'clock	**las tres**
	las tr*es*
four o'clock	**las cuatro**
	las cw*a*tro
in the morning	**de la mañana**
	deh la man-yanna
in the afternoon ⎤	**de la tarde**
in the evening ⎦	deh la t*a*rdeh
at night	**de la noche**
	deh la n*o*ch-eh
It's ...	**Es ...**
	es ...
noon	**mediodía**
	med-yo-d*ee*a
midnight	**medianoche**
	med-ya-n*o*ch-eh
It's ...	**Son ...**
	son ...
five past five	**las cinco y cinco**
	las th*i*nko ee th*i*nko
ten past five	**las cinco y diez**
	las th*i*nko ee dee-*e*th
a quarter past five	**las cinco y cuarto**
	las th*i*nko ee cw*a*rto
twenty past five	**las cinco y veinte**
	las th*i*nko ee b*e*ynteh
twenty-five past five	**las cinco y veinticinco**
	las th*i*nko ee beyntee-th*i*nko
half past five	**las cinco y media**
	las th*i*nko ee med-ya
twenty-five to six	**las seis menos veinticinco**
	las s*e*ys men-os beyntee-th*i*nko

twenty to six	**las seis menos veinte**
	las seys men-os beynteh
quarter to six	**las seis menos cuarto**
	las seys men-os cwarto
ten to six	**las seis menos diez**
	las seys men-os dee-eth
five to six	**las seis menos cinco**
	las seys men-os thinko
At what time (does the train leave)?	**¿A qué hora (sale el tren)?**
	ah keh ora (sal-eh el tren)
At ...	**A las ...**
	ah las ...
13.00	**trece**
	treth-eh
14.05	**catorce cero cinco**
	cat-ortheh thairo thinko
15.10	**quinze diez**
	kin-theh dee-eth
16.15	**dieciséis quince**
	dee-ethee-seys kintheh
17.20	**diecisiete veinte**
	dee-ethee-see-et-eh beynteh
18.25	**dieciocho veinticinco**
	dee-ethee-ocho beynteh-thinko
19.30	**diecinueve treinte**
	dee-ethee-nweb-eh treynta
20.35	**veinte treinta y cinco**
	beynteh treynta ee thinko
21.40	**veintiuna cuarenta**
	beyntee-oona cwa-renta
22.45	**veintidós cuarenta y cinco**
	beyntee-dos cwa-renta ee thinko
23.50	**veintitrés cincuenta**
	beyntee-tres thin-cwenta
0.55	**cero cincuenta y cinco**
	thairo thin-cwenta ee thinko
in ten minutes	**en diez minutos**
	en dee-eth minootos
in a quarter of an hour	**en un cuarto de ora**
	en oon cwarto deh ora
in half an hour	**en media hora**
	en med-ya ora
in three quarters of an hour	**en tres cuartos de hora**
	en tres cwartos deh ora

DAYS

Monday	**lunes**
	loon-es
Tuesday	**martes**
	mart-es
Wednesday	**miércoles**
	mee-aircol-es
Thursday	**jueves**
	hweb-es
Friday	**viernes**
	bee-airn-es
Saturday	**sábado**
	sabad-o
Sunday	**domingo**
	domingo
last Monday	**el lunes pasado**
	el loon-es pasad-o
next Tuesday	**el martes próximo**
	el mart-es proxim-o
on Wednesday	**el miércoles**
	el mec-aircol-es
on Thursdays	**los jueves**
	los hweb-es
until Friday	**hasta el viernes**
	asta el bee-airn-es
before Saturday	**antes del sábado**
	ant-es del sabad-o
after Sunday	**después del domingo**
	despwes del domingo
the day before yesterday	**anteayer**
	anteh-ayair
two days ago	**hace dos días**
	ath-eh dos dee-as
yesterday	**ayer**
	ayair
yesterday morning	**ayer por la mañana**
	ayair por la man-yanna
yesterday afternoon	**ayer por la tarde**
	ayair por la tardeh
last night	**la noche pasada**
	la noch-eh pasad-ah
today	**hoy**
	oy

this morning	**esta mañana**
	esta man-y*a*nna
this afternoon	**esta tarde**
	esta t*a*rdeh
tonight	**esta noche**
	esta n*o*ch-eh
tomorrow	**mañana**
tomorrow morning ⟧	man-y*a*nna
tomorrow afternoon	**mañana por la mañana**
	manyan-a por la man-y*a*nna
tomorrow evening	**mañana por la tarde**
	man-y*a*nna por la t*a*rdeh
tomorrow night	**mañana por la noche**
	man-y*a*nna por la n*o*ch-eh
the day after tomorrow	**pasado mañana**
	pas*a*d-o man-y*a*nna

MONTHS AND DATES

January	**enero**
	en-*air*o
February	**febrero**
	feb-r*air*o
March	**marzo**
	m*a*rtho
April	**abril**
	abr*i*l
May	**mayo**
	m*a*-yo
June	**junio**
	h*oo*n-yo
July	**julio**
	h*oo*l-yo
August	**agosto**
	a-g*o*sto
September	**septiembre**
	sept-y*e*mbreh
October	**octubre**
	oct*oo*breh
November	**noviembre**
	nob-y*e*mbreh
December	**diciembre**
	dith-y*e*mbreh

in January	**en enero**
	en en-*airo*
until February	**hasta febrero**
	*a*sta feb-*rairo*
before March	**antes de marzo**
	*a*nt-es deh m*a*rtho
after April	**después de abril**
	despw*e*s deh abr*i*l
during May	**durante mayo**
	doo-r*a*nteh m*a*-yo
not until June	**hasta junio no**
	*a*sta h*oo*n-yo no
the beginning of July	**principios de julio**
	printh*i*p-yos deh h*oo*l-yo
the middle of August	**mediados de agosto**
	med-y*a*d-os deh ag*o*sto
the end of September	**finales de septiembre**
	fin-*a*l-es deh sept-y*e*mbreh
last month	**el mes pasado**
	el mes pas*a*do
this month	**este mes**
	*e*steh mes
next month	**el mes próximo**
	el mes pr*o*xim-o
in spring	**en primavera**
	en preema-b*ai*ra
in summer	**en verano**
	en beh-r*a*n-o
in autumn	**en otoño**
	en ot*o*n-yo
in winter	**en invierno**
	en imb-y*ai*rno
this year	**este año**
	*e*steh *a*n-yo
last year	**el año pasado**
	el *a*n-yo pas*a*d-o
next year	**el año próximo**
	el *a*n-yo pr*o*xim-o
in 1982	**en mil novecientos ochenta y dos**
	en m*i*l nobeh-thee-*e*ntos ochenta ee d*o*s
in 1985	**en mil novecientos ochenta y cinco**
	en m*i*l nobeh-thee-*e*ntos ochenta ee th*i*nko

in 1990	**en mil novecientos noventa**	
	en mil nobeh-thee-entos nobenta	
What's the date today?	**¿Qué fecha es hoy?**	
	keh fech-ah es oy	
It's the 6th of March	**Es el seis de marzo**	
	es el seys deh martho	
It's the 12th of April	**Es el doce de abril**	
	es el doth-eh deh abríl	
It's the 21st of August	**Es el veintiuno de agosto**	
	es el beyntee-oono deh agosto	

Public holidays

● On these days, offices, shops and schools are closed.

1 January	**Año Nuevo**	New Year's Day
6 January	**Epifania**]	Epiphany
	Día de Reyes	
19 March	**San José**	St Joseph's Day
...	**Jueves Santo**	Maundy Thursday
...	**Viernes Santo**	Good Friday
...	**Día de la Ascensión**	Ascension Thursday
	Corpus Christi	Corpus Christi Day
1 May	**Día del Trabajo**	Labour Day
25 July	**San Jaime**]	St James's Day
	Día de Santiago	
15 August	**Día de la Asuncion**	Assumption Day
12 October	**Día del Pilar**]	Columbus Day
	Fiesta de la Hispanidad	
1 November	**Todos los Santos**	All Saints Day
8 December	**Inmaculada Concepción**	Immaculate Conception Day
25 December	**Navidad**	Christmas Day

COUNTRIES AND NATIONALITIES

Countries

Australia	**Australia**	
	owstral-ya	
Austria	**Austria**	
	owstr-ia	
Belgium	**Bélgica**	
	bel-heeca	
Britain	**Gran Bretaña**	
	gran bret-an-ya	

Canada	**Canadá**
	canad*a*
East Africa	**Africa del Este**
	*a*frica del *e*steh
Eire	**Eire**
	*a*ireh
England	**Inglaterra**
	ingla-t*e*rra
France	**Francia**
	fr*a*nth-ya
Greece	**Grecia**
	gr*e*th-ya
India	**India**
	*i*ndia
Italy	**Italia**
	it*a*l-ya
Luxembourg	**Luxemburgo**
	looxemb*o*org-o
Netherlands	**Los Paises Bajos**
	los pa-*ee*s-es b*a*-hos
New Zealand	**Nueva Zelanda**
	nw*e*b-ah th*e*l-*a*nda
Northern Ireland	**Irlanda del Norte**
	eer-l*a*nda del n*o*rteh
Pakistan	**Pakistán**
	pakist*a*n
Portugal	**Portugal**
	portoog*a*l
Scotland	**Escocia**
	escoth-ya
South Africa	**Sudáfrica**
	sood-*a*frica
Spain	**España**
	esp*a*n-ya
Switzerland	**Suiza**
	sw*ee*tha
United States	**Estados Unidos**
	est*a*d-os oon*ee*dos
Wales	**Gales**
	g*a*l-es
West Germany	**Alemania occidental**
	al-emm*a*n-ya ok-theeden-t*a*l
West Indies	**Antillas**
	ant*ee*-yas

Nationalities

American	**americano/americana**
	americano/americana
Australian	**australiano/australiana**
	owstral-yan-o/owstral-yan-ah
British	**británico/británica**
	britan-ico/britan-ica
Canadian	**Canadiense**
	canad-yen-seh
East African	**africano/africana del este**
	africano/ africana del esteh
English	**inglés/inglesa**
	in-gles/in-gles-ah
Indian	**Hindú**
	in-doo
Irish	**irlandés/irlandesa**
	eerland-es/eerland-es-ah
a New Zealander	**neozelandés/neozelandesa**
	neo-thel-and-es/neo-thel-and-es-ah
a Pakistani	**pakistaní**
	pakistanee
Scots	**escocés/escocesa**
	escoth-es/escoth-es-ah
South African	**sudafricano/sudafricana**
	sood-africano/sood-africana
Welsh	**galés/galesa**
	gal-es/gal-es-ah
West Indian	**antillano/antillana**
	anti-yan-o/anti-yan-ah

DEPARTMENT STORE GUIDE

Alfombras	Carpets
Alimentación	Food
Artículos de deporte	Sports
Artículos de limpieza	Cleaning materials
Artículos de montaña	Mountaineering department
Artículos de piel	Leather goods
Artículos de playa	Beach accessories
Artículos de viaje	Travel articles
Baterías de cocina	Kitchen utensils
Blusas	Blouses
Bolsos	Bags
Bricolage	Do it yourself
Caballeros	Menswear
Cafetería	Café
Caja	Checkout
Camisas	Shirts
Camisería	Shirt department
Camping	Camping
Cinturones	Belts
Cojines	Cushions
Confecciones	Ready-made clothing
Corbatas	Ties
Cortinas	Curtains
Cosméticos	Cosmetics
Cristalería	Glassware
Cuarto/Cuarta	Fourth
Cubiertas	Coverlets
Discos	Records
Droguería	Toiletries
Electrodomésticos	Electric appliances
Fajas	Girdles
Ferretería	Hardware
Fotografía	Photography
Guantes	Gloves
Hogar	Home furnishing
Información	Information
Jardinería	Garden
Jerseys	Pullovers
Joyería	Jewellery
Juguetes	Toys
Laminados	Laminates
Lencería	Lingerie

Librería	Books
Loza	Earthenware
Mantas	Blankets
Mantelerías	Table linen
Medias	Stockings
Mercería	Haberdashery
Moda juvenil	Young fashion
Modas señora	Ladies fashions
Muebles	Furniture
Muebles de cocina	Kitchen furniture
Niños/Niñas	Children
Oportunidades	Special offers
Pañería	Drapery
Papelería	Stationery
Perfumería	Perfumery
Piso	Floor
Planta	Floor
Planta baja	Ground floor
Porcelana	China
Primero	First
Radio	Radio
Reclamaciones	Complaints
Regalos	Gifts
Relojería	Watches
Retales	Materials
Ropa confeccionada	Ready-made clothing
Ropa de cama	Bedding
Ropa infantil	Children's wear
Ropa interior	Underwear
Sección	Department
Segundo	Second
Señora/Señoras	Ladies' Wear
Sombrerería	Millinery
Sostenes	Bras
Sótano	Basement
Sujetadores	Bras
Tapicerias	Furnishing fabrics
Televisión	Television
Tercero	Third
Vajilla	Crockery
Ventas a crédito	Accounts
Zapatería	Footwear
Zapatillas	Slippers

CONVERSION TABLES

Read the centre column of these tables from right to left to convert
from metric to imperial and from left to right to convert from
imperial to metric e.g. 5 litres = 8.80 pints; 5 pints = 2.84 litres.

pints		litres		gallons		litres
1.76	1	0.57		0.22	1	4.55
3.52	2	1.14		0.44	2	9.09
5.28	3	1.70		0.66	3	13.64
7.07	4	2.27		0.88	4	18.18
8.80	5	2.84		1.00	5	22.73
10.56	6	3.41		1.32	6	27.28
12.32	7	3.98		1.54	7	31.82
14.08	8	4.55		1.76	8	36.37
15.84	9	5.11		1.98	9	40.91

ounces		grams		pounds		kilos
0.04	1	28.35		2.20	1	0.45
0.07	2	56.70		4.41	2	0.91
0.11	3	85.05		6.61	3	1.36
0.14	4	113.40		8.82	4	1.81
0.18	5	141.75		11.02	5	2.27
0.21	6	170.10		13.23	6	2.72
0.25	7	198.45		15.43	7	3.18
0.28	8	226.80		17.64	8	3.63
0.32	9	255.15		19.84	9	4.08

inches		centimetres		yards		metres
0.39	1	2.54		1.09	1	0.91
0.79	2	5.08		2.19	2	1.83
1.18	3	7.62		3.28	3	2.74
1.58	4	10.16		4.37	4	3.66
1.95	5	12.70		5.47	5	4.57
2.36	6	15.24		6.56	6	5.49
2.76	7	17.78		7.66	7	6.40
3.15	8	20.32		8.65	8	7.32
3.54	9	22.86		9.84	9	8.23

miles		kilometres
0.62	1	1.61
1.24	2	3.22
1.86	3	4.83
2.49	4	6.44
3.11	5	8.05
3.73	6	9.66
4.35	7	11.27
4.97	8	12.87
5.59	9	14.48

A quick way to convert kilometres to miles: divide by 8 and multiply by 5. To convert miles to kilometres: divide by 5 and multiply by 8.

fahrenheit (°F)	centigrade (°C)		lbs/ sq in	k/ sq cm
212°	100°	boiling point	18	1.3
100°	38°		20	1.4
98.4°	36.9°	body temperature	22	1.5
86°	30°		25	1.7
77°	25°		29	2.0
68°	20°		32	2.3
59°	15°		35	2.5
50°	10°		36	2.5
41°	5°		39	2.7
32°	0°	freezing point	40	2.8
14°	–10°		43	3.0
–4°	–20°		45	3.2
			46	3.2
			50	3.5
			60	4.2

To convert °C to °F: divide by 5, multiply by 9 and add 32. To convert °F to °C: take away 32, divide by 9 and multiply by 5.

CLOTHING SIZES

Remember – always try on clothes before buying. Clothing sizes are usually unreliable.

women's dresses and suits

Europe	38	40	42	44	46	48
UK	32	34	36	38	40	42
USA	10	12	14	16	18	20

men's suits and coats

Europe	46	48	50	52	54	56
UK and USA	36	38	40	42	44	46

men's shirts

Europe	36	37	38	39	41	42	43
UK and USA	14	$14\frac{1}{2}$	15	$15\frac{1}{2}$	16	$16\frac{1}{2}$	17

socks

Europe	38–39	39–40	40–41	41–42	42–43
UK and USA	$9\frac{1}{2}$	10	$10\frac{1}{2}$	11	$11\frac{1}{2}$

shoes

Europe	34	$35\frac{1}{2}$	$36\frac{1}{2}$	38	39	41	42	43	44	45
UK	2	3	4	5	6	7	8	9	10	11
USA	$3\frac{1}{2}$	$4\frac{1}{2}$	$5\frac{1}{2}$	$6\frac{1}{2}$	$7\frac{1}{2}$	$8\frac{1}{2}$	$9\frac{1}{2}$	$10\frac{1}{2}$	$11\frac{1}{2}$	$12\frac{1}{2}$

Do it yourself

Some notes on the language

This section does not deal with 'grammar' as such. The purpose here is to explain some of the most obvious and elementary nuts and bolts of the language, based on the principal phrases included in the book. This information should enable you to produce numerous sentences of your own making.

There is no pronunciation guide in this section, partly because it would get in the way of the explanations and partly because you have to do it yourself at this stage if you are serious – work out the pronunciation from all the earlier examples in the book.

THE

All nouns in Spanish belong to one of two genders: masculine or feminine, irrespective of whether they refer to living beings or inanimate objects.

The (singular)	masculine	feminine
the address		la dirección
the apple		la manzana
the bill		la cuenta
the cup of tea		la taza de té
the glass of wine	el vaso de vino	
the key		la llave
the luggage	el equipaje	
the menu	el menú	
the newspaper	el periódico	
the receipt	el recibo	
the sandwich	el bocadillo	
the suitcase		la maleta
the telephone directory		la guía telefónica
the timetable	el horario	

Important things to remember

- *The* is **el** before a masculine noun and **la** before a feminine noun.
- You can often tell if a singular noun is masculine or feminine by its ending. Masculine nouns usually end in 'o' and feminine nouns in 'a'. However there are several exceptions notably a whole group of nouns which end in 'e' e.g. **el equipaje,** so you should try to learn and remember all genders. If you are reading a word with **el** or **la** in front of it, you can detect its gender immediately: **el menú** is masculine (*m.* in dictionaries) and **la dirección** is feminine (*f.* in dictionaries).
- Does it matter? Not unless you want to make a serious attempt to speak correctly and scratch beneath the surface of the language. You would be understood if you said **la menú** or even **el dirección,** providing your pronunciation was good.

The (plural)	masculine	feminine
the addresses		**las direcciones**
the apples		**las manzanas**
the bills		**las cuentas**
the cups of tea		**las tazas de té**
the glasses of wine	**los vasos de vino**	
the keys		**las llaves**
the luggage (this is only singular in Spanish, see above)		
the menus	**los menús**	
the newspapers	**los periódicos**	
the receipts	**los recibos**	
the sandwiches	**los bocadillos**	
the suitcases		**las maletas**
the telephone directories		**las guías telefónicas**
the timetables	**los horarios**	

Important things to remember

- As a general rule, a noun adds an 's' to become plural. However, a noun ending in a consonant adds 'es' e.g. **la dirección, las direcciones.**
- *The* is **los** before masculine nouns in the plural.
- *The* is **las** before feminine nouns in the plural.

Practise saying and writing these sentences in Spanish:

Have you got the key?	Tiene usted la llave?
Have you got the luggage?	Tiene usted ... ?
Have you got the telephone directory?	
Have you got the menu?	
I'd like the key	Quiero la llave
I'd like the receipt	Quiero ...
I'd like the bill	
I'd like the keys	
Where is the key?	¿Dónde está la llave
Where is the timetable?	¿Dónde está ... ?
Where is the address?	
Where is the suitcase?	
Where is the luggage?	
Where are the keys?	¿Dónde están las llaves?
Where are the sandwiches?	¿Dónde están ... ?
Where are the apples?	
Where are the suitcases?	
Where can I get the key?	¿Dónde puedo obtener la llave?
Where can I get the address?	¿Dónde puedo obtener ... ?
Where can I get the timetables?	

Now make up more sentences along the same lines.
Try adding please: por favor, at the end.

A/AN

A/an (singular)	masculine	feminine
an address		una dirección
an apple		una manzana
a bill		una cuenta
a cup of tea		una taza de té
a glass of beer	un vaso de vino	
a key		una llave
a menu	un menú	
a newspaper	un periódico	
a sandwich	un bocadillo	
a suitcase		una maleta
a telephone directory		una guía telefónica
a timetable	un horario	

Some/any (plural)	masculine	feminine
addresses		unas direcciones
apples		unas manzanas
bills		unas cuentas
cups of tea		unas tazas de té
glasses of wine	unos vasos de vino	
keys		unas llaves
luggage	unos equipajes	
menus	unos menús	
newspapers	unos periódicos	
receipts	unos recibos	
sandwiches	unos bocadillos	
suitcases		unas maletas
telephone directories		unas guías telefónicas
timetables	unos horarios	

Important things to remember

- *A* or *an* is **un** before masculine nouns and **una** before feminine nouns.
- The plural, *some* or *any* is **unos** before masculine nouns and **unas** before feminine nouns.
- In certain Spanish expressions, **unos** and **unas** are left out:

See an example of this in the sentences marked * below.

Practise saying and writing these sentences in Spanish:

Have you got a receipt?	¿Tiene usted ... ?
Have you got a menu?	
I'd like a telephone directory	Quiero ...
I'd like some sandwiches	
Where can I get some newspapers?	¿Dónde puedo obtener ... ?
Where can I get a cup of tea?	
Is there a key?	¿Hay una llave?
Is there a timetable?	¿Hay ... ?
Is there a telephone directory?	

Is there a menu?	
Are there any keys?	¿Hay unas llaves?
Are there any newspapers?	¿Hay ... ?
Are there any sandwiches?	

Now make up more sentences along the same lines.
Then try these new phrases:
Tomo ... (I'll have ...)
Necesito ... (I need ...)

I'll have a glass of wine	**Tomo un vaso de vino**
I'll have some sandwiches	**Tomo ...**
I'll have some apples	
I need a cup of tea	**Necesito una taza de té**
I need a key	**Necesito ...**
* I need some keys	**Necesito llaves**
* I need some addresses	**Necesito ...**
* I need some sandwiches	
* I need some suitcases	

SOME/ANY

In cases where *some* or *any* refer to more than one thing, such as *some/any ice-creams* and *some/any apples,* **unos** and **unas** are used as explained earlier:
unos helados (some/any ice-creams)
unas manzanas (some/any apples)
As a guide, you can usually *count* the number of containers or whole items.

In cases where *some* refers to part of a whole thing or an indefinite quantity in English, there is no Spanish equivalent. Just leave it out.

Look at the list below:

the beer	la cerveza	some beer	cerveza
the bread	el pan	some bread	pan
the butter	la mantequilla	some butter	mantequilla
the cheese	el queso	some cheese	queso

The same would apply to the following words

the coffee	el café	the sugar	el azúcar
the flour	la harina	the tea	el té
the lemonade	la limonada	the water	el agua
the oil	el aceite	the wine	el vino

Practise saying and writing these sentences in Spanish:

Have you got some coffee?	¿Tiene usted café?
Have you got some flour?	
Have you got some sugar?	
I'd like some butter	Quiero mantequilla
I'd like some oil	
I'd like some bread	
Is there any lemonade?	¿Hay limonada?
Is there any water?	
Is there any wine?	
Where can I get some cheese?	¿Dónde puedo obtener queso?
Where can I get some flour?	
Where can I get some water?	
I'll have some beer	Tomo cerveza
I'll have some tea	
I'll have some coffee	

THIS AND THAT

There are two words in Spanish
   esto (this)
   eso (that)
If you don't know the Spanish for an object, just point and say:

Quiero eso	I'd like that
Tomo esto	I'll have that
Necesito esto	I need this

HELPING OTHERS

You can help yourself with phrases such as:

I'd like ... a sandwich	**Quiero ... un bocadillo**
Where can I get ... a cup of tea?	**¿Donde puedo obtener ... una taza de té?**
I'll have ... a glass of beer	**Tomo ... un vaso de vino**
I need ... a receipt	**Necesito ... un recibo**

If you come across a compatriot having trouble making himself or herself understood, you should be able to speak to the Spanish person on their behalf.

Note that it is not necessary to say the words for he (él), she (ella) and I (yo) in Spanish unless you want to emphasize them e.g. *He'll* have a beer and *I'll* have a glass of wine.

He'd like ...	**(Él) quiere un bocadillo**
	(el) kee-*air*eh oon boccad*ee*-yo
She'd like ...	**(Ella) quiere un bocadillo**
	el-ya kee-*air*eh oon boccad*ee*-yo
Where can he get ... ?	**¿Dónde puede (él) obtener una taza de té?**
	dondeh pwed-eh (el) obten-*air* oona t*a*th-a deh teh
Where can she get ... ?	**¿Dónde puede (ella) obtener una taza de té?**
	dondeh pwed-eh (el-ya) obten-*air* oona t*a*th-a deh teh
He'll have ...	**(Él) toma un vaso de vino**
	(el) tom-a oon b*a*sso deh b*ee*no
She'll have ...	**(Ella) toma un vaso de vino**
	(el-ya) tom-a oon b*a*sso deh b*ee*no
He needs ...	**(Él) necesita un recibo**
	(el) neth-es*ee*ta oon reth*ee*bo
She needs ...	**(Ella) necesita un recibo**
	(el-ya) neth-es*ee*ta oon reth*ee*bo

You can also help a couple or a group if they are having difficulties. The Spanish word for *they* is ellos (men) and ellas (women), and ellos (men and women) but it is usually left out altogether. Look at the verb ending:

They'd like ...	**(Ellos) quieren queso**
	(el-yos) kee-*air*en kes-o
They'd like ...	**(Ellas) quieren queso**
	(el-yas) kee-*air*en kes-o

Where can they get . . . ?	**¿Dónde pueden obtener mantequilla?** dondeh pwed-en obten-*air* mantehk*ee*-ya
They'll have . . .	**Toman vino** tom-an b*ee*no
They need . . .	**Necesitan agua** neth-es*ee*tan *a*gwa

What about the two of you? No problem. The word for *we* is nosotros (men) nosotras (women), but it is only really important to change the verb.

We'd like . . .	**Queremos vino** keh-rem-os b*ee*no
Where can we get . . . ?	**¿Dónde podemos obtener agua?** dondeh pod-em-os obten-*er* *a*gwa
We'll have . . .	**Tomamos cerveza** tom-*a*m-os thairbeth-a
We need . . .	**Necesitamos azúcar** neth-esectam-os athoocar

Try writing out your own checklists for these four useful phrase starters, like this:

Quiero . . .	Queremos . . .
Quiere (él) . . .	Quieren (ellos) . . .
Quiere (ella) . . .	Quieren (ellas) . . .
Dónde puedo obtener . . . ?	Dónde . . . obtener . . . ?
Dónde puede (él) obtener . . . ?	Dónde . . . (ellos) obtener . . . ?
Dónde pueden (ellas) obtener . . . ?	Dónde . . . (ellas) obtener . . . ?

MORE PRACTICE

Here are some more Spanish names of things. See how many
different sentences you can make up, using the various points of
information given earlier in this section.

		singular	plural
1	ashtray	cenicero (m)	ceniceros
2	bag	bolsa (f)	bolsas
3	car	coche (m)	coches
4	cigarette	cigarrillo (m)	cigarrillos
5	corkscrew	sacacorchos (m)	sacacorchos
6	garage (repairs)	garaje (m)	garajes
7	grapes	uva (f)	uvas
8	ice-cream	helado (m)	helados
9	knife	cuchillo (m)	cuchillos
10	melon	melón (m)	melones
11	passport	pasaporte (m)	pasaportes
12	postcard	tarjeta postal (f)	tarjetas postales
13	salad	ensalada (f)	ensaladas
14	shoe	zapato (m)	zapatos
15	stamp	sello (m)	sellos
16	station	estación (f)	estaciones
17	street	calle (f)	calles
18	sunglasses		gafas de sol (f)
19	telephone	teléfono (m)	teléfonos
20	ticket	billete (m)	billetes

Index

Ken Welsh
Hitch-Hiker's Guide to Europe

The new and completely updated edition of this
invaluable guide covers Europe, North Africa and the
Middle East. Ken Welsh gives advice on routes to take,
what to take, eating, sleeping, local transport, what to see,
together with information on currency, useful phrases and
working abroad.

'Hitch-hikers will adopt it as their travelling bible but
it's amusing and informative for those who fancy more
traditional ways'   BBC

edited by Harriet Peacock
The Alternative Holiday Catalogue

If you're looking for a holiday that you won't find in a
travel agent's window . . . if there's something you've
always wanted to try your hand at . . . or if you want to
take your special interest on holiday with you, this
A–to–Z of ideas and information is the book you need.
150 different types of special interest holiday, from
backgammon and Bible study to Zen, upholstery and
giving up smoking. This book tells you where to go,
what to take, what it costs, and what you'll find when
you get there.

John Slater
Just Off for the Weekend
Slater's hotel guide

The bestselling author of *Just Off the Motorway* has
selected more than a hundred places to stay, with
details of what to see and walks to take, specially
recommended pubs and restaurants – and all within a
Friday evening's drive from one of England's big cities.
With an introduction by Anna Ford.

Harrap's New Pocket French and English Dictionary

The classic French/English and English/French reference for students and travellers, this edition contains some 4,500 entries in each language, including all the principal words in current use – recent additions to both languages, scientific terms, tourist expressions. Entries also contain phonetic renderings and examples of idiomatic usage.

A Multilingual Commercial Dictionary

Some 3,000 words and phrases in common commercial use are listed in English, French, German, Spanish and Portuguese followed by their translation in the other languages. The equivalent American expression is also included where relevant. Simple to use and invaluable for everyday reference, the dictionary covers terms used throughout banking, accounting, insurance shipping, export and import and international trade.

Arthur Eperon
Traveller's Italy

A whole variety of holiday routes to guarantee that you eat, drink, explore and relax in the places the Italians themselves would choose. The best places to sample local speciality foods and wines, spectacular scenery, facts the history books won't tell you, as well as the magnificent beaches and art treasures you'd expect. Arthur Eperon is one of the best-known travel writers in Europe and has an extensive knowledge of Italy and its food and wine. With an introduction by Frank Bough.

Arthur Eperon
Traveller's France

Six major routes across France, taking in the best
restaurants and hotels, visiting the most interesting
out-of-the-way places. This detailed and up-to-the-
minute handbook is for the traveller who wants more
out of France than a mad dash down the motorway.
Each of the six routes across the country is illustrated with
a specially-commissioned two-colour map, and includes
a host of information on where to eat and drink, where
to take children, where to stay, and how to get the most
out of the towns and countryside.

John Slater
Just Off the Motorway

The new and enlarged edition of a sensational bestseller.
Introduced by Russell Harty.

Here's the new, bang-up-to-date edition of the handbook
everyone needs. Detailed research, careful sampling,
and more than 150 maps show where you can find any
service you require – cheaper and better – by turning off
at a junction and driving no more than three miles
off the motorway – eating, drinking, overnight stops,
breakdown services, petrol, visits.

' Worth a detour to buy it'   DAILY MAIL